Apartments, Townhouses and Condominiums

Apartments, Townhouses and Condominiums

edited by

Elisabeth Kendall Thompson FAIA
Senior Editor
Architectural Record

An Architectural Record Book

McGraw-Hill Book Company

New York   St. Louis   San Francisco   Auckland
Düsseldorf   Johannesburg   Kuala Lumpur
London   Mexico   Montreal   New Delhi
Panama   Paris   São Paulo   Singapore
Sydney   Tokyo   Toronto

Library of Congress Cataloging in Publication Data
Thompson, Elisabeth Kendall, comp.
    Apartments, townhouses, and condominiums.
    Originally published in 1958 under title:
Apartments and dormitories, and entered under:
Architectural record.
    Articles, originally published in Architectural record.
    "An Architectural record book."
    Includes index.
    1. Apartment houses. 2. Row houses.
3. Condominium (Housing)   I. Architectural record.
Apartments and dormitories.   II. Architectural record.
III. Title.
NA7860.A7 1975   728.'31   74-26665
ISBN 0-07-002321-2

567890 HDHD 798

The editors for this book were Jeremy Robinson and Hugh S.
Donlan. The designer was Elaine Gongora. It was set in Op-
tima by Progressive Typographers.

Printed and bound by Halliday Lithograph Corporation.

Contents

Preface

This book makes its appearance at a time when multi-unit housing—the apartment building, garden complex or town-house—is of increasing importance on the American scene, both because of the waning incidence of the single-family house, for so long the prevailing type of dwelling in this country, and because of the continuing and pressing need for more housing—a need that can now be met only by some form of multi-unit solution.

The new emphasis on multi-unit buildings is the result of many factors, not the least of which are the population pressures of the last ten to twenty years and the change in the composition of the population to a preponderance of young (under 30) and old (over 60) people. But by far the greatest influence in this change has been the spiralling cost of land which has made the single-family house all but prohibitive in cost, and has led inevitably to the more intensive use of each plot of land, most often to guarantee a desired investment return.

To most Americans, "intensive use of land" and "density" are terms whose immediate connotation is an undesirable condition. Yet neither term in itself carries a qualitative meaning but is, rather, quantitative. Whether density is "good" or "bad" depends on how the density is achieved, and what effect it has on the surrounding area and on the town or city as a whole. A well-designed project of considerable density, if conceived with grace and dignity and a concern for high human values, can produce an environment for living whose amenity is of enviable quality; if conceived only with the cynical aim of making money fast and

with no concern for human values, the environment that results will have no amenity, however low the density.

It takes imagination, ingenuity and great dedication to bring off a project of real design quality, within a realistic budget, and with a fair return on the cost of the land and of construction. But it is possible, and the projects selected for inclusion in this book justify that assertion. The architects and the developers who brought these projects to actuality had courage and imagination, and one hopes that the wide circulation that their publication here will give them will serve to encourage others to equal or surpass in quality what they have shown can be done.

The work of many people has gone into the production of this book, and thanks are due to them all, for contributions large and small that have made the book possible. Particular acknowledgment is due my colleagues on the staff of *Architectural Record* who, in addition to myself, were the writers and editors on these projects when they appeared in the magazine, for there their work has almost always appeared anonymously: Herbert L. Smith, managing editor; senior editor Mildred Schmertz; assistant editors Barclay Gordon and Charles Hoyt; and editorial assistant Janet Nairn, to whom I owe additional thanks for her invaluable help in compiling the index of this volume. It goes without saying that none of the book's contents would have been possible without the overall contribution of Walter Wagner, editor-in-chief of *Architectural Record*.

Elisabeth Kendall Thompson

Apartments and Townhouses in the City

Most city people live in apartments or in row houses, and would not find it "city living" to live in anything else. Indeed, much of the character that connotes a city derives from these distinctly and historically urban building types. Today's apartment buildings vary in size and height, in kinds of unit, and in plan, and tend to provide, even in lower-rent examples, more amenities than their predecessors—even those of fifty years ago—but the principle on which they are based is still the same, and more important than ever today: city land is costly and must be used with care and economy for housing that is convenient, accessible and attractive. In this section are projects chosen to show the variety of solution that illuminates the descriptive term "urban."

Low Rise Buildings

Zoning laws set up restrictions on height of apartment buildings in certain kinds of residential neighborhoods, as they do on number of units, required parking, and other aspects of multi-unit buildings. But even more important is the unspoken and unwritten requirement that the new building in the neighborhood respect the scale of the existing buildings and that it be appropriate as a new element. The low-rise apartment building has an urban character of its own, with its own kind and degree of amenity, from the interior court with its landscaping, fountains and pools, to its ingenious handling of interior spaces. What kind of character it turns to the passerby depends on the size of the city in which it is located: Northpoint (pages 14–15) could only be in a large and populous place; Lemon Tree Village (pages 2–3) belongs in the small town where it is. In between these extremes are large and small buildings in large and small cities: variety, choice, urban living at a human scale.

Wray Studio photos

1 Many attempts, says architect Charles Harrison Pawley, were made to rezone this small parcel of land in Coconut Grove, Florida for high-rise development. Land costs seemed to indicate that was necessary but the municipality resisted on the grounds that such construction would ruin the residential quality of the neighborhood. Working within the limits of the local zoning code, however, Pawley found he could place 20 low-rise units on the property, 1.45 acres in area, based on a planned unit development concept. The placement had to be much more random than usual in this case because of the large oak and banyan trees growing on the site. Even though the ten duplex buildings are identical, their unusual positioning and use of courts and walls which respond to the entourage make the whole

seem like a village, not multi-family housing. Thus the name of this handsome project: Lemon Tree Village.

The houses themselves are quite straightforward. Using common Florida construction methods, Pawley's design was built in 1972 for $20.00 per sq ft, making the cost for each 1250 sq ft unit $25,000, including air conditioning, carpeting and all appliances. The unit plans have no interior partitions as such; all the walls are part of the concrete block structure, gaining stability from returns that form closets and other recesses. A flat slab concrete deck, sprayed with an acoustical texture material where exposed as ceiling, ties the walls together. One of each pair of units has only a single bedroom and bath upstairs with the remaining area used as a sundeck. The other house has

two bedrooms and baths on the second floor. Both bedrooms have access to a covered balcony (right). The interior walls have a smooth plaster finish while on the exterior, a sprayed stucco with white marble aggregate was used. The resulting forms, with cantilevered balconies and roofs (above), and with all flashing and trim painted white, are reminiscent of early Bauhaus work. Yet lovingly set among the sinuous tree trunks and dappled with the shadows of branches and leaves, they take on a richness and complexity that completely belies their simple means.

LEMON TREE VILLAGE, Coconut Grove, Florida. Architect: *Charles Harrison Pawley.* Engineers: *McGlinchy and Pundt.* Landscaping: *Jim Talley.* Interior designers: *T.L.S. Designs* and *Dennis Jenkins.* Builder and owner: *Nicholas G. Polizzi.*

FIRST FLOOR   SECOND FLOOR   5

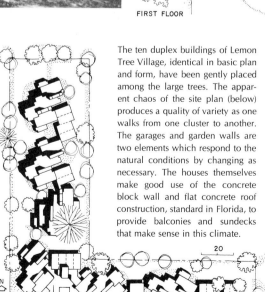

The ten duplex buildings of Lemon Tree Village, identical in basic plan and form, have been gently placed among the large trees. The apparent chaos of the site plan (below) produces a quality of variety as one walks from one cluster to another. The garages and garden walls are two elements which respond to the natural conditions by changing as necessary. The houses themselves make good use of the concrete block wall and flat concrete roof construction, standard in Florida, to provide balconies and sundecks that make sense in this climate.

20

N

2

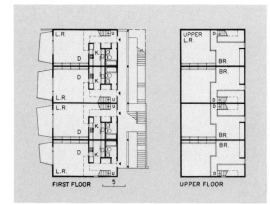

FIRST FLOOR   5   UPPER FLOOR

This simply-massed four-story frame structure in Seattle, located on a narrow lot that drops 40 feet in its 100-foot length, contains eight duplex units. On each pair of floors are four units, similar except that the upper apartments are slightly larger since they overhang the common corridor on the third floor. These units also have sloping ceilings and balconies. One unit (occupied by the archi-tect) has a private balcony.

On the exterior, the floor levels are expressed by horizontal boards, a strong contrast to the vertical grooves of the plywood siding. Simple detailing, sheet materials and standard windows and doors contributed to an economic solution.

EIGHT APARTMENT UNITS, Seattle, Washington. Architect: *George C. Oistad, Jr.* Contractor: *Omar Brown.*

Vern Green photos

The architect's own apartment combines interesting spaces with bold graphics and other handsome furnishings. The entry hall, with its simple straightforward wood stair, leads directly to the airy living-dining room. The upper floor, open to living room, provides light and ventilation from both sides for the bedroom.

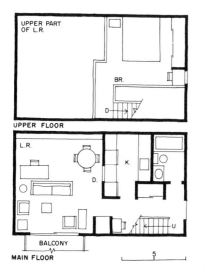

UPPER PART
OF L.R.

BR.

D.

UPPER FLOOR

L.R.

K.

D.

BALCONY

MAIN FLOOR

5

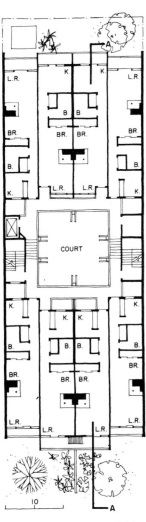

Convenient access is provided for all apartments by elevator or stairs. White-painted stucco panels are used as a foil for the extensive areas of redwood on the exterior; interiors are painted gypsum board on wood studs.

3 Twenty-five studio apartments have been deftly organized in the low-rise structure on a 50-by-137.5-foot lot. Though the high cost of land necessitated the number of apartments, the use of courts and balconies throughout gives each unit an unusual sense of openness for such an urban set-ting—the site is within walking distance of downtown San Fran-cisco.

The trim, sophisticated design reflects both its citified character, and the lightness and ins-and-outs of upper-story bays, set on heavier foundations, that typify the neigh-boring older buildings. Even the vertical rods of the balcony rail-ings echo those of the traditional and required fire escapes. Along with these elements, red brick paving, redwood siding and care-fully planned landscaping are used within the limits of the budget to provide a warm, human "Bay Region" character.

Jeremiah O. Bragstad photos

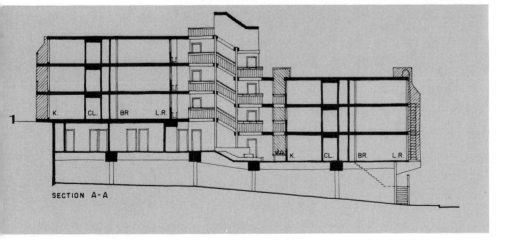

SECTION A-A

The structure has three to four levels of wood frame construction (it follows the upward slope of the site) over one level of concrete-framed parking garage. The main entrance is up a broad flight of stairs and through a brick-paved, grille-gated entrance into the court.

The garden area within is a strongly patterned arrangement of brick walks, terraces and concrete planters and pools. Banks of flower boxes carry the sense of garden up to all levels. Though small, the apartments contain all the desirable amenities, including fireplaces.

STUDIO APARTMENTS, San Francisco, California. Owner: *Rollin E. Meyer.* Architects: *Whisler/Patri Associates—Carl Wisser,* project architect. Engineers: *Degenkolb & Associates.* Landscape architect: *Edward Jenilli.* Acoustical engineer: *Roger Maineri.* Contractor: *Rolin E. Meyer Company.*

Hickey & Robertson photos

4 These extremely pleasant apartments offer great individuality and privacy in an apparently random (but actually carefully controlled) arrangement of units. Maximum use of the relatively limited ground area of the half-round site contributed to the interesting "in and out" relationship between the forms of the 10 units, which were added to an existing apartment development. Throughout, modest and economic materials were combined to create an atmosphere of some style. The architect and owner, Howard Barnstone, comments that, "privacy, the watchword of so many garden apartments, was taken into much consideration with the privately walled courts on the interior of the circle. But privacy sometimes palls, so the kitchens and some bedrooms are opened to the street."

VASSAR PLACE APARTMENTS, Houston, Texas. Owner: *Howard Barnstone.* Architects: *Howard Barnstone & Partners.* Builder: *Metropolitan Builders Company.*

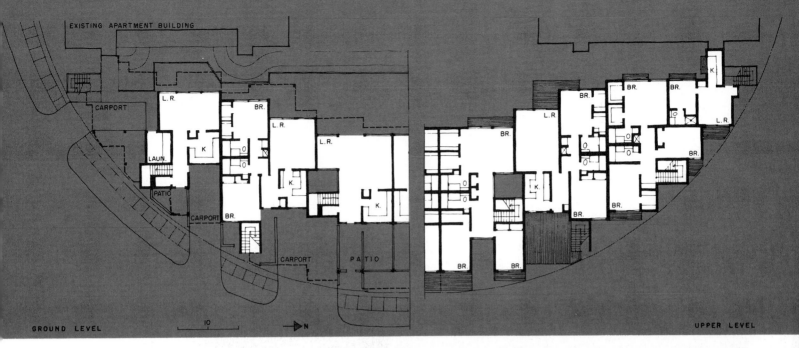

In a linked community of apartments (the half-plans shown continue around the site in mirror image), Barnstone has sought to keep the neighborhood from becoming overly stratified by incorporating a range of apartment sizes and rents, from a small efficiency unit to a 2,100-square-foot, three-bedroom, three-bath, two-story townhouse. All of the units are replete with balconies, decks, and courts at back and front—and occasionally in the center. The structure is wood frame, with painted, striated plywood exteriors and plasterboard and plywood interiors. Floors are surfaced with vinyl asbestos or sisal matting. Each apartment has been provided with individual heating and air-conditioning units.

The parking structure, which meets local off-street parking requirements, is the heart of the scheme for the town. The seven units in the center of the site are built upon it, while the other units, half a level lower, face away from it toward the street. Typical unit plans, for both two- and three-bedroom models, show the compactness of the design.

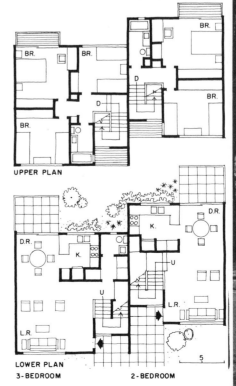

UPPER PLAN

LOWER PLAN

3-BEDROOM   2-BEDROOM

5

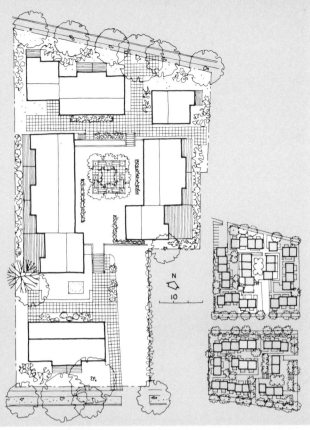

5

These seventeen townhouses, the first stages of two larger groups, were conceived to serve the special needs of student families (usually with children), to blend into the surrounding single-family neighborhood, and to be adaptable to rental if necessary.

The architects met with the students and their wives who would be occupying the houses in order to understand their particular needs. Those meetings indicated that the families preferred two-story houses with no neighbors above or below. Children are more free to move about and their parents can retreat to the master bedroom to study. The architect specified carpets and drapes in rich colors which help unify furnishings of diverse origin.

The site planning, with houses built around and on top of a parking structure for 30 cars, unifies the handsome houses into a pleasant community. Once again, much thought has been given to children's activities. They can run all around the site or play on the tile-paved plaza above the garage. The houses built adjacent to it give this space an intimate scale.

The houses are sheathed in vertical redwood, a traditional Bay Area material, and have anodized aluminum windows.

JOHN R. LITTLE RESIDENCES, San Anselmo, California. Owner: *San Francisco Theological Seminary*. Architects: *Frants Albert* and *William W. Abend* of *HCD Collaborative*. Engineers: *T. Y. Lin, Kulka, Yang and Associates* (structural), *Yanow and Bauer* (mechanical). Landscape architect: *Lisa Guthrie*. Contractor: *Elvin C. Stendell, Inc.*

Alan Stiles photos

6 Few of the small apartment buildings built on leftover lots in every American city recently can be considered architectural contributions to their neighborhoods. Peters and Clayberg and Associates of San Francisco were most successful, while satisfying their developer/client's goals of rentability and low construction cost, in relating their design to the scale of the tree-lined street. The 17-unit building is in an area of Oakland that, because of its proximity to the downtown and to major traffic arteries, is rapidly changing from single- to multi-family housing. Another of the site's advantages is access to views of San Francisco and the Bay as well as of downtown Oakland. Thus, almost all of the apartments have their balconies and bay windows oriented toward them. In addition, a

small court at the rear of the site offers the possibility of cross-ventilation for many of the units. Seven of them also have wood-burning fireplaces.

Perhaps the most interesting aspect of the building is its structure. A ground-level garage of concrete and concrete block, which takes care of all off-street parking requirements, supports the three stories and penthouse of wood frame construction above. Adequate protection against fire was necessary, of course. A heavy-duty water line with valves on the landings of the open stairwells (above) and fire extinguishers in the glazed corridor (above right) are two types easily seen. The most obvious expression of the lightweight construction is the redwood plywood siding. It was chosen, say the architects, not just because it compared fa-

vorably in cost with the stucco so often used for such buildings in California, but because it complemented the mature trees nearby. It is finished with a semi-transparent stain that contrasts with the darker-stained horizontal and vertical trim. The plywood is used in the lobby (right) for a wall sculpture of numbers including the building's address, which was executed by the architects themselves. The lobby is entered, as is the garage, adjacent to the open stairwell.

HARRISON STREET APARTMENTS, Oakland, California. Architects: *Peters and Clayberg and Associates—Tom Caulfield,* project architect. Engineer: *Robert Vandenbosch.* Landscape architects and interior designers: *Peters and Clayberg and Associates.* Owner and builder: *Barry S. Slatt.*

The 17-unit building nestles onto a slightly sloping lot of less than 7000 sq. ft. Access to most of the apartments is along a corridor glazed with steel industrial sash painted red-orange. Apartments look into a small inner court which provides cross-ventilation for some of the units. All apartments have balconies, most of which take advantage of interesting views across San Francisco Bay.

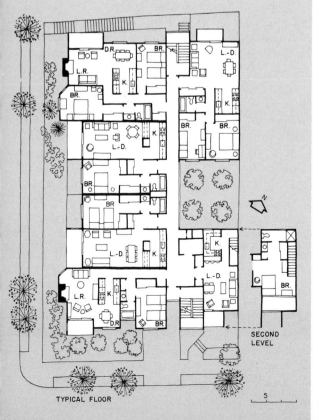

TYPICAL FLOOR

SECOND LEVEL

5

7

Although garden apartments are usually located in suburban areas, Northpoint was deliberately located in a city with the intent of providing the same amenities that suburban locations offer along with the advantages of city living. Northpoint is in the North Waterfront area of San Francisco, within walking distance of shops and restaurants and with good public transportation to other parts of the city. Its four landscaped courts, each developed for a different kind of use, are unusual in urban apartments: two have swimming pools, the others have fountains; all have trees and grass and places for quiet relaxation. In addition, most units have semi-private outdoor space, either enclosed patios or balcony decks. There are 12 lobbies for entrance to the apartments, a device which conveys a sense of small scale despite the large number of apartments and density of site use. Of the 514 units, 233 are one bedroom and 14 are two bedroom units. Parking is underground, one stall to a tenant, with direct elevators to apartments. Next to the buildings is a block-size commercial development by the same developers and architects.

NORTHPOINT APARTMENTS, San Francisco, California. Owner and developer: *Gerson Bakar and Associates*. Architects: *Wurster, Bernardi & Emmons*. Engineers: *David A. Welisch* (structural), *Atlas Heating and Ventilating* (mechanical), *Edward Shinn & Associates* (electrical). Landscape architects: *Lawrence Halprin & Associates*. Interior design: *Matt Kahn*. Contractor: *Williams & Burrows, Inc.*

Photos by Robert Brandeis

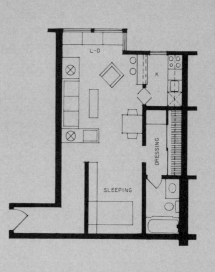

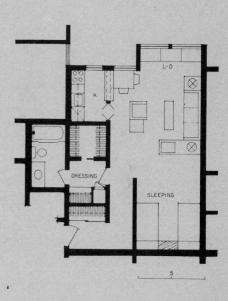

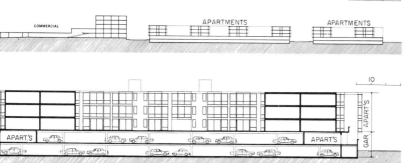

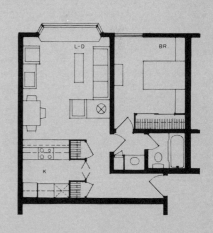

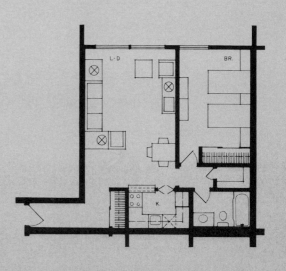

8

The site is in an area of Berkeley, California in process of transitional zoning changes from single-family dwellings to new apartment projects. Zoning laws permitted eight units on the 40-foot-wide lot, but the architect and the owner agreed that four were as many as could be used without destroying the neighborhood scale. The solution reflects the traditional scale and materials found in the surrounding houses.

As can be seen in the plan, two buildings face each other in mirror image fashion across a private entry deck, access to which is from a side walkway. Working with a rather small space, the architect has achieved a feeling of spaciousness in the interiors by using shed roofs, and glass walls overlooking a tightly landscaped area. Automobiles are parked under the front building and in a parking forecourt.

APARTMENT, Berkeley, California. Architects: *Lee & Roberson—Eugene Lew,* project designer, Contractor: *Ambrose Construction Company.*

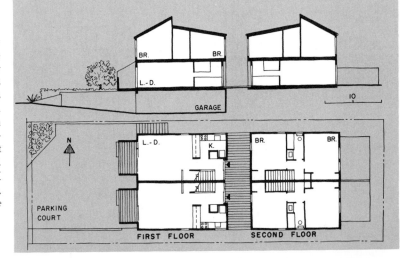

Glenn Mitchell photos

Chuck Crandall photos

9 Esplanade Village steps down a 1.2-acre suburban site near Redondo Beach, California to form an unusually handsome 105-unit rental community overlooking the ocean. Careful planning and massing has resulted in an orderly plan with eight apartment variations: 20 per cent efficiencies, 40 per cent one-bedroom, 20 per cent two bedroom. A maximum number are oriented toward the ocean but all have views and the privacy of individual units has been maintained with considerable care.

The massing seeks to emphasize the repetitive character of the system while investing the whole project with a pleasant village character and scale. Grade circulation is through a sequence of small courts—or an esplanade—with lateral circulation on bridges overhead. Shared facilities include a pool, a recreation room on the downhill side of the project, and a two-level subterranean garage.

The rental market in the area dictated the use of a three-story wood frame construction (Type V) with a one-hour fire rating. Exterior walls have a sprayed-on plaster finish, patios and open corridors are fitted with metal railings and sloped roofs are finished in asphalt shingle. Standard components and details are employed throughout.

But in spite of the simple construction, the rigorous ordering of forms and the fairly substantial densities, Esplanade Village has a very inviting character. Part of it results from the openness of stairs and corridors and the outdoor lifestyle these elements imply. More of it, perhaps, is due to the careful siting and massing that create, in the mind of resident and passerby alike, an important sense of place and also of community.

ESPLANADE VILLAGE, Redondo Beach, California. Owner: *Esplanade Village Ltd.* Architects: *Brent, Goldman, Robbins & Bown—Dean Bell,* project architect. Structural engineers: *Ismail & Wagner.* Contractor: *Alter Building Co.*

The site is bounded on two sides by public roads and dips twenty-five feet between roads. The project is designed to be expansible as adjacent 40-foot lots become available. At present, Esplanade Village includes 82,000 square feet of net rental area at densities of approximately 89 units per acre.

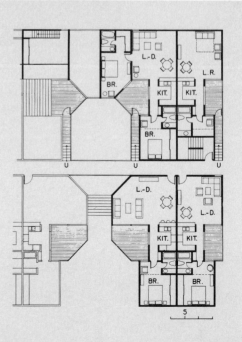

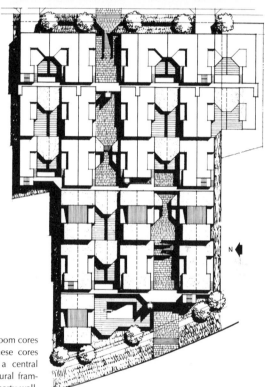

Similar kitchen and bathroom cores are used throughout. These cores are backed up against a central party wall with all structural framing perpendicular to the party wall.

High Rise Buildings

In metropolitan centers, where land is both scarce and expensive, tall apartment buildings make economic sense. But since they affect the city's skyline as well as the pedestrian's eyeline, they need to make visual sense too. Height and bulk, shape and form, details and materials determine its role in the city. One will be suavely untraditional, like Lake Point Tower in Chicago (pages 22–27); another will subtly recognize a strong regional heritage, as does John Fewkes Tower, also in Chicago (pages 32–35). Interior planning must have the excellence to sell or rent the apartment; exterior appearance will specify its acceptance—or rejection—in the city.

1

Skyscrapers are seldom surrounded by space these days, and only rarely can be viewed from near and far and many directions as Lake Point Tower can. Presently the world's tallest apartment building, it stands off by itself on a spit of land which juts into Lake Michigan at Navy Pier Park near the intersection of Lake Shore Drive and Grand Avenue in Chicago's Near North Shore. Given such a site, it is fortunate for the Chicago skyline that the form of this 65-floor, 900-unit cloverleaf-shaped apartment tower stands up so well to scrutiny, and that the play of reflections on its handsome bronze-toned aluminum and glass sheath rewards the onlooker at all hours of the day in every kind of light.

A dream of Mies
In 1921 the late Mies van der Rohe made his first sketches and models for a skyscraper office building with a curving glass curtain wall. Designed in an irregular shape for an imaginary site (see model photo) it prefigured Lake

Point Tower by 47 years. Construction of the concrete skeleton of the apartment tower and installation of its curtain wall was completed early last year in Mies' adopted city—the world's most appropriate place for the first fulfillment of an old skyscraper dream.

. . . by two Miesian disciples
George Schipporeit and John Heinrich, young architects who once worked with Mies, are the first men to build a skyscraper with a curtain wall of this type and Lake Point Tower was their first real commission.

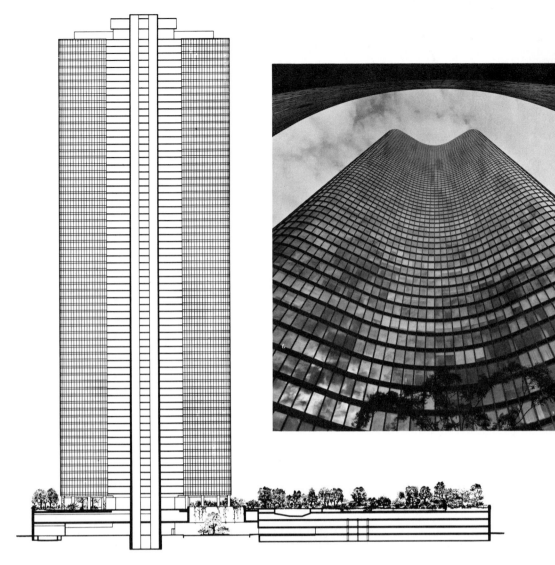

A tower and podium scheme

From the beginning the architects urged the tall tower concept to conserve as much private park and recreation space adjacent to living space as possible. To the right of the base are four levels of parking for 700 cars. To the left, directly under the tower, are two floors of commercial space. Rising through the center to the full height of the building is the triangular-shaped structural core containing elevators, stairwells, corridor supply ducts and the main electrical distribution systems. It is designed to withstand all horizontal moments and shear forces. Only vertical compressive forces are transmitted through the columns to the caissons. At the top of the building are the two penthouse levels. The lower penthouse houses the elevator equipment rooms and ventilation fans. The upper penthouse is a restaurant.

The aerial photo shows the podium functions. The large circular opening brings daylight to the entrance drive below which serves the garage, the main lobby, the commercial space, a health club and indoor pool, a loading dock and receiving rooms. The main refrigerated rubbish collection point connected with the rubbish chute is incorporated under the podium as part of the loading dock. At the garden level of the podium, directly behind the arcade, are enclosed community rooms. The arcade overlooks the garden.

PLAZA LEVEL PLAN

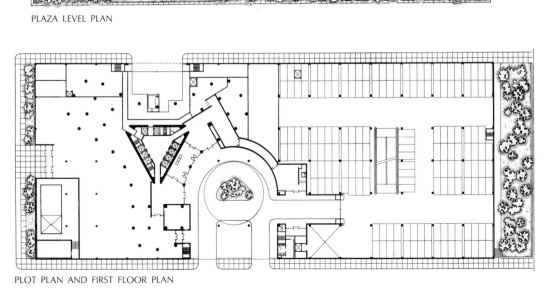

PLOT PLAN AND FIRST FLOOR PLAN

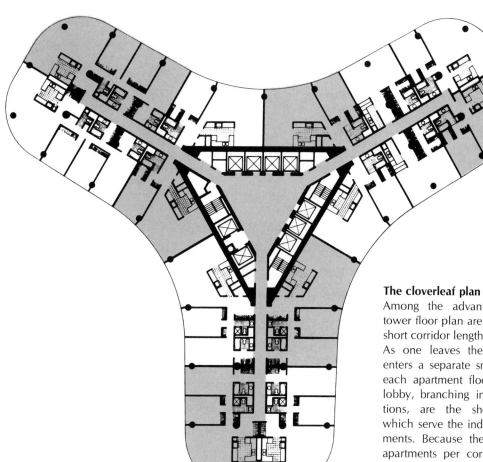

COMPOSITE FLOOR PLAN

The cloverleaf plan

Among the advantages of the tower floor plan are the relatively short corridor lengths it generates. As one leaves the elevator he enters a separate small lobby at each apartment floor. From this lobby, branching in three directions, are the short corridors which serve the individual apartments. Because there are fewer apartments per corridor, a high degree of privacy for each apartment in each wing has been achieved. One sees that the maximum number of apartments flanking each corridor is six. This occurs on floors which have a one-bedroom, efficiency, one-bedroom configuration. On floors having two-bedroom units, and those having the one-bedroom, three-bedroom configuration, the maximum number of apartments flanking the corridor is four. The two-bedroom unit established the basic module of a scheme which permits the building owners at low cost to quickly increase and decrease apartment types to meet the demands of a changing real estate market. The plan reveals that to change two of the latter units into one three-bedroom and one single-bedroom unit, all that is necessary is to move the party wall one-half bay over, thus incorporating the bedroom from the adjacent apartment along with its bath. Moving the party walls one bay in each direction forms two one-bedroom units flanking a single efficiency unit. In this instance one bath becomes a kitchen. Pipe space and shafts need not be changed.

Climate control

Heating and air-conditioning units for bedrooms, living and dining spaces have been coordinated with the window wall components, eliminating the central system and its space-consuming distribution requirements. Public lobbies are heated by duct heaters, and cooling is supplied from the 69th floor mechanical penthouse which supplies both heating and cooling to the corridors. HVAC units are mounted in cabinet units and slide forward to make the controls accessible. Next to these are similar cabinets with lift-up lids which admit fresh air through grilles located just below the fixed sash, as can be seen in the section.

LAKE POINT TOWER, Chicago, Illinois. Owner: *Hartnett-Shaw & Associates, Inc.* and *Fluor Properties*. Architects: *Schipporeit-Heinrich, Inc.;* associate architects: *Graham, Anderson, Probst & White*. Mechanical engineer: *William Goodman*. Landscape architect: *Alfred Caldwell*. Contractor: *Crane Construction Co.*

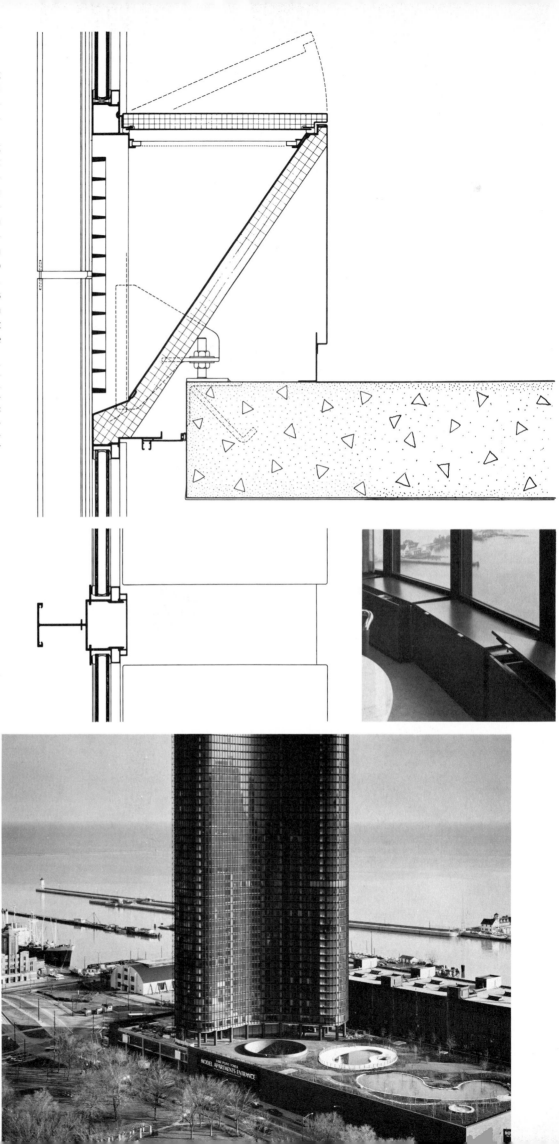

2 Tower and garden apartments are combined in this group with remarkable skill to achieve an unusual degree of seclusion and, at the same time, openness. The tower rises to a height of 15 stories from the reinforced concrete bearing piers which surround the elevator lobby at entrance level. The one-story garden apartments are ranged along the sides of the almost square site, and are entered from the court in which the tower stands. The entrance level of the site—151 feet by 150 feet—is used to capacity, yet the tower remains free, with light and air on all sides. The concrete shear walls of the tower cantilever from the building core, and act as partitions between and within apartments and as enclosing exterior around the garden units;

textured architectural concrete for the piers and shear walls. Spandrels are of black aluminum. A full level under the entire site provides for a parking garage and for all services. Located just north of the University of Chicago Midway Plaisance, the building was designed to house personnel from the university.

FIFTEENTH FLOOR

5825 DORCHESTER, Chicago. Owner: *Draper and Kramer, Inc.;* Architects and engineers: *Skidmore, Owings & Merrill—William E. Hartmann, partner-in-charge; Bruce J. Graham, partner in charge of design; Richard E. Lenke, associate partner and project manager; Robert Diamant, associate partner and senior designer; S. H. Iyengar, project structural engineer; Albert I. Cho, project mechanical engineer.* Landscape architect: *Stephanie Kramer.* General contractor: *Turner Construction Company.*

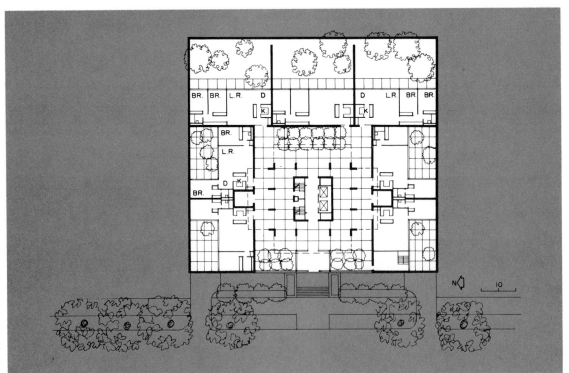

Cantilevered floor slabs of tower building make a sheltered approach through the court to garden apartment entrances. Each of the six two-bedroom garden apartments (and a one-bedroom unit for the superintendent) has its own walled garden off which its rooms open.

The broad band of windows floods all tower rooms with daylight. Living room is a nice 13 by 20 feet in size; dining room, which opens off it, is 12 by 13 feet. Typical floor plan shows use of shear walls for partitions and enclosing walls. The tower contains 28 three- and four-bedroom apartments.

TYPICAL FLOOR

3 Great vertical tiers of broad bay windows
—borrowed from Chicago's brilliant late-
nineteenth-century architectural past—
dominate the four façades of this 30-story
apartment tower by Harry Weese. "Chicago School" buffs will be reminded of
Holabird and Roche's Tacoma Building
begun in 1887; Burnham and Root's Mon-
adnock Building and William Le Baron
Jenney's Manhattan Building, both finished
in 1891; Burnham and Company's Reli-
ance Building of 1894; and several other
Chicago skyscrapers of that great decade
for which, as in Weese's building, fenestration was everything.

Weese decided upon a square tower
with a capacity limited to eight units per
floor to allow multiple orientation and
cross ventilation for each apartment, and
for as many individual rooms as possible.
The building corridors on each floor have
windows at opposite ends, the extensions
of which light the apartment kitchens as
shown in the typical floor plan on the
next page.

In addition to the foregoing advantages, the tower scheme also provides short
corridors (extending only 29 feet on either
side of the elevators), conserves the site
and, as a slender vertical mass, does not
overwhelm its neighboring townhouses as
a lower, bulkier structure might. The tower,
which contains 224 apartments in all, is
perched on top of a two-level 88-car
garage and parking area shielded behind a
grass berm.

Costs were tightly controlled to keep
rents within the reach of retired teachers,
for whom the building was constructed by
its owners, the Chicago Teachers Union.
The entire building is of typical concrete
flat-slab construction with 8-inch non-
bearing masonry walls faced with a light-
colored brick.

Deep vertical recesses in each principal side of the building add counter-emphasis to the projecting bay windows, provide daylight for corridors and kitchens, and define the canopied entrances. In deliberate contrast, each secondary façade of the building has been made flatter. In the typical floor plan two basic units (shaded) are repeated. As shown on the plot plan the roof of the two-level garage serves as a landscaped plaza.

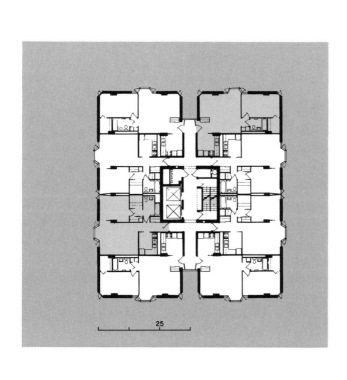

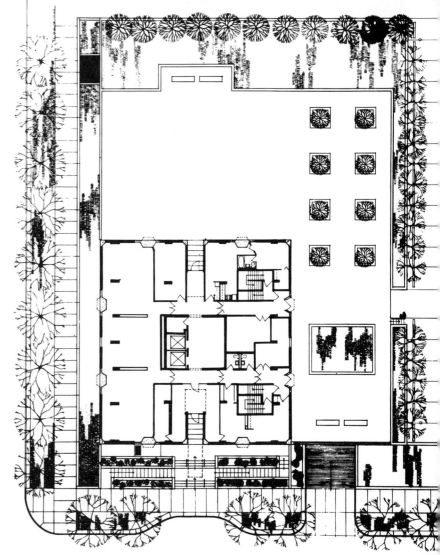

A typical living room interior (above) shows three of the five segments of the window unit. One segment brings light to the adjoining bedroom on the opposite side of the wall. The other is concealed by the curtain just visible to the right. Weese repeats the bay window silhouette in the corridor partitions.

JOHN FEWKES TOWER, Chicago, Illinois. Architects: *Harry Weese & Associates.* Engineers: *The Engineers Collaborative* (structural); *S. R. Lewis & Associates* (mechanical/electrical). Landscape architects: *Office of Dan Kiley.* Consultants: *Dolores Miller & Associates* (interiors); *Kodaras & Associates* (acoustical engineers). Contractor: *Morris Handler Co.*

4 Kennedy Plaza is a project of New York State's Urban Development Corporation. Its prominent location in the downtown district and the height of its lower building in the generally low-rise city of Utica would alone make it a focal point, but pleasantly open site and handsome buildings assure its importance in and to the city.

The best part of the apartments from the tenants' viewpoint is the balconies. The UDC did not ask for balconies in their program, but Franzen was able to provide rather large ones for every unit; all are at least 55 square feet in area, inset for privacy between neighbors, and accessible by large sliding glass doors off the living rooms.

Franzen's intention here was to break up the façades of his buildings and break up the lengths of their corridors in order to make both more humane in scale, less boring and less easy to comprehend than "boxes." This is accomplished by sliding the apartments out of line with each other in plan and carefully inserting the balconies; the internal organization

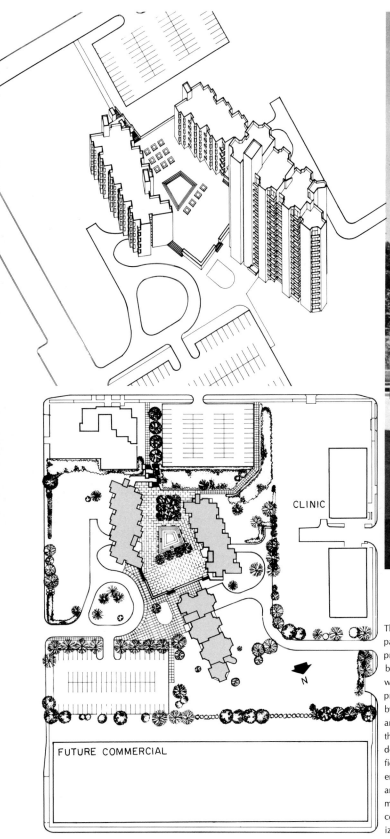

CLINIC

FUTURE COMMERCIAL

N

The site plan (left) shows ample parking (two units per one car). The project is two blocks from the main business section, and some tenants will obviously walk to work. The project is surrounded on two sides by older single-family residences, and there was some opposition to the project from these Utica residents. Franzen, as well as UDC officials, were on local television several times explaining the project, and there were many community meetings. An advisory council of community leaders was also organized by the UDC (as in most of the

of the apartments very definitely generates the façades.

All of the apartments in both low-rise sections have two bedrooms; the 17-story tower is made up of zero- and one-bedroom units. In spite of the intricacy of its planning, there are no great structural tricks at Kennedy Plaza. The buildings are the simplest possible flat-plate concrete frame with a masonry skin wall.

But the masonry *is* interesting, being laid up with a special adhesive mortar that is stronger than even the brick in tension, if mixed properly. This allows large brick panels to be laid up on the ground and lifted into place, as happened with some of the walls on this project. Or, the masonry units can be placed in the usual way. There is no moisture penetration through this mortar, so with Kennedy Plaza, the walls are built with a dense four-inch brick which allows no moisture penetration either, and cavity walls have been eliminated. This special mortar is one technological innovation UDC has been experimenting with on many of its projects, to speed construction time and cut costs. The other principal technical experiment of UDC's—one used here at Kennedy Plaza—is a single-stack plumbing system that does not require a second pipe running alongside the main waste line. The second pipe is required in ordinary plumbing for ventilation of internal pressures within the system. Instead, a patented self-aerating fitting is placed wherever a fixture waste pipe meets the main stack, and a special de-aerator fitting is used in the basement.

George Cserna photos

areas where they build) to help strengthen the dialogue and determine needs.

The three buildings are placed on the site to help enclose the central plaza (photos left, above), which has a fountain in the center planned for children to play in. The two five-story units have nearly identical floor plans, with only their entrances shifted. On the next page, a furnished two-bedroom unit is shown set up by the developers for prospective tenants. Also shown is the ground floor lobby.

The UDC has found this system generally economical, and it seems possible to reduce the usual amount of piping and fittings by at least one-half.

Franzen has tried to make this housing durable with concrete and masonry, and to reduce the hardness of these materials through contrasting site planning and the intricacy of his forms. Today the plaza, which is the focus of the design, is becoming livelier as the tenants begin using it for sitting, wading and an occasional softball game. As the trees and shrubbery grow, this will help, too; the most important thing is that the residents so far seem to like living in the newest building in town.

KENNEDY PLAZA, Utica, New York. Owners: *The Urban Development Corporation.* Architects: *Ulrich Franzen & Associates—Samuel Nylen,* associate-in-charge. Engineers: *Aaron Garfinkel & Associates* (structural); *Benjamin & Zicherman* (mechanical). Developer: *CDC Utica Inc.* Contractor: *Sofarelli Associates.*

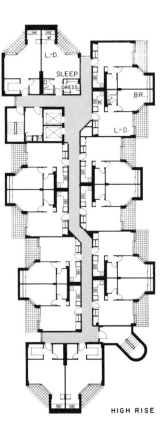

HIGH RISE

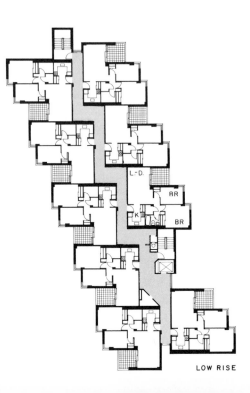

LOW RISE

5

Coleman Towers is located on a hill-side site in Stamford, Connecticut, and automobile access is by a winding drive that brings cars in under the building where unloading can take place under cover. The building contains 88 units with from one to three bedrooms and, on the lower floors, a child care center, meeting room and professional offices. As a result of savings in the structure (which uses precast concrete floor slabs and brick facing) it was possible to include air conditioning and carpeting in the apartments. Coleman Towers is the first of several 221(d)3 projects that the architect has helped nonprofit sponsors to get built. In this case, he not only persuaded Clairol, Inc., a national corporation based in Stamford, to provide seed money so that planning could begin, but he was instrumental in getting needed zoning changes so that the project could be built.

COLEMAN TOWERS, Stamford, Connecticut. Architect: *Robert L. Wilson.* Engineers: *Schupack & Associates* (structural); *Tizian Engineering Associates* (mechanical); *Parsons, Bromfield & Redniss* (site). Landscape architect: *Robert L. Wilson.* Contractor: *Winston A. Burnett Construction Company.*

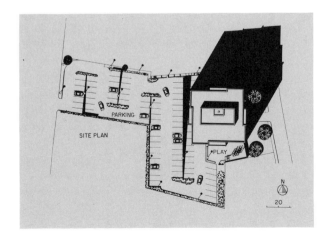

SITE PLAN

PARKING

PLAY

N 20

TYPICAL FLOOR

N 10

Townhouses

Townhouses may be the city's most variable housing type: a few units along a shaded court, many in a block-square development; two-story, three-story, even four-story units; a wide range of materials. Some have the small-town look though they are in the big city; but few try to look big-city in a small town. The townhouse (once called the row house) suggests an urban condition in a never-never time, but it satisfies, as no other city housing does, the longing for individuality, even when it is obvious only in the color of the entrance door. Here are examples of townhouses from the East Coast to the West Coast, from Texas, Oklahoma, and the Midwest—wood, stucco, brick, shingle: a different approach to urban living.

1

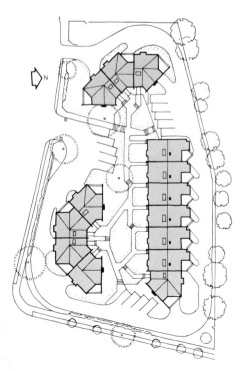

Two blocks from downtown Greenwich, Connecticut, a town that has never really opened its arms to contemporary architecture, Rogers Moore and Associates have designed fourteen condominium units that blend remarkably well in scale and detail with the neighborhood. But the Meadgate Condominiums are not just warmed-over suburbia. Within walking distance of the railroad station, the project is intended for couples about to retire who want to stay in Greenwich but who no longer need a large house in the country. Stringent zoning laws determined much of the planning for the site, formerly an old YWCA. Parking and driveway requirements, including 1:1 guest parking, necessitated the sunken perimeter drive and the basement garages. A carefully detailed promenade in the center of the site is the focus for the entrances and living rooms of all the units. Several mature trees have been integrated into the landscape design and give it a settled quality. The houses (there are two basic schemes) have either two or three bedrooms and have large central skylights which fill the interior with light.

MEADGATE CONDOMINIUMS, Greenwich, Connecticut. Architects: *Rogers Moore and Associates—Allen Moore, Jr., John B. Rogers, James M. McConnell.* Engineers: *Engineers Design Group* (structural); *Swanson Associates* (mechanical/electrical). Landscape architect: *William Rutherford.* Landscape consultant: *Carol R. Johnson.* Developer: *Patterson Condominium Corp.* Contractor: *Deluca Construction Company.*

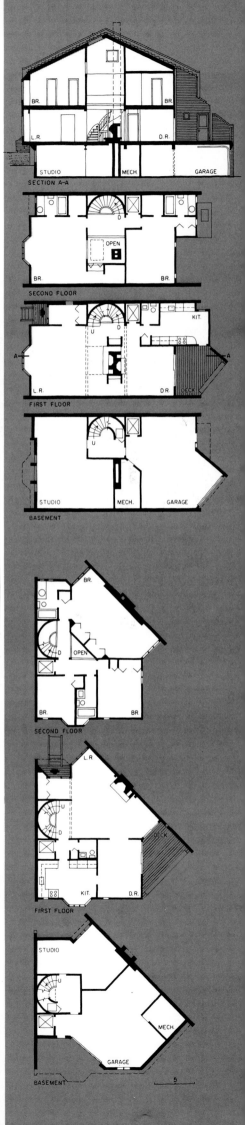

Winding staircases, freestanding brick fireplaces, bay windows, and elevators are features of the two basic plans that were used to fit fourteen units onto the tightly restricted one-and-a-half acre site. Each house also has a built-in garage. Although the complex focuses on an interior landscaped mall, the buildings have well captured much of the scale and feeling of the existing neighborhood.

SECTION A-A

SECOND FLOOR

FIRST FLOOR

BASEMENT

STUDIO   MECH.   GARAGE

SECOND FLOOR

FIRST FLOOR

BASEMENT

Jonas Dovydenas

2 Six spacious condominium townhouses set on three building lots—less than a quarter-acre—on Chicago's near North Side represent the best kind of urban renewal. Their red brick and dark mortar walls blend into a neighborhood of three- and four-story nineteenth-century masonry buildings with remarkable ease.

The site plan originally proposed by architects Booth and Nagel, opposite page, shows seven houses. The design is based on a 5-foot 6-inch module, expressed on the ground floor in the photo above. They suggested three units, each four-modules wide near the street, and four three-module units behind. Ultimately three four-module units were built to the rear instead. The narrower

houses, otherwise identical, had only two bedrooms on the second floor.

The entry court, delightful between the two rows of houses, permits a doubling of the original lot density without making the houses at the back seem less desirable. Although each of the houses occupies only half the amount of land an old-fashioned Chicago townhouse did, the amount of space inside is sizable by today's standards—2,350 square feet.

Compact planning of stairs and rooms with plumbing in the center of each floor, permits major rooms to have maximum exposure to the outdoors. All of the living rooms especially benefit. Running parallel to the garden, they have an openness

that the living rooms in the houses they replaced could never have. And change in floor level permits living room ceilings as high as those in the most stately old house.

A unique feature is the top floor studio and its completely private roof terrace. Including the walled gardens and entry court at ground level; almost 75 per cent of the site area is available for outdoor activities even though 50 per cent more people live on the land now.

————————————————

TOWNHOUSES, Chicago, Illinois. Owners: *Jared Shlaes & Co./Urban Associates of Chicago.* Architects: *Booth & Nagle.* Engineers: *Weisinger-Holland Ltd.* (structural); *Wallace and Migdal, Inc.* (mechanical). Interior designer: *Jody Kingrey.* Contractor: *Inland Construction Co.*

THIRD FLOOR

ROOF TERR.

STUDIO

SECOND FLOOR

BR. BR.

BR.

FIRST FLOOR 5

COURTYARD

L.R.

K

D.R.

BASEMENT

STOR.

UT.

REC. RM.

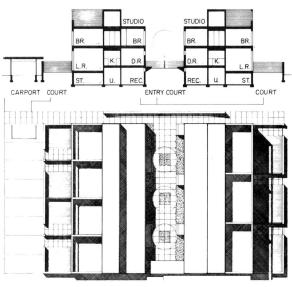

STUDIO STUDIO

BR. BR. BR. BR.

L.R. K D.R. D.R. K L.R.

ST. U. REC. REC. U. ST.

CARPORT COURT ENTRY COURT COURT

The section shown illustrates how the building height is minimized in the relatively narrow central entry court, while to the street and back alley it is maximized by the terrace structure to relate to taller neighboring buildings.

3

These three townhouses (a two-story unit, flanked by two single-story ones) are unusually effective and elegant examples of the spaciousness and livability that can be achieved on a small urban lot. Though built as a promotional development to examine the uses and potential of steel in house construction (and steel is used throughout as structure, furniture, equipment and fittings), the design goes further, to demonstrate that material's compatibility with such other materials as wood, terrazzo, travertine, brick and stucco, to create comfortable, warmly attractive homes.

All the houses are quite introverted for privacy and have walled-in entrance courts. Other courts are sprinkled through the plans for added light and openness to the interiors. The family automobile entrance to each house is at the back, with a sheltered two-car parking space flanking a public alley.

In all the houses the partitioning (and, in the two-story house, the upper floor) is planned to give basic visual privacy, yet permit the eye to travel beyond for longer vistas.

The structure of the houses is steel post and beam on concrete slabs. Roofs are steel decking, surfaced with built-up roofing (and a small wood-slat roof deck on one house). Exteriors are stucco and red cedar louvers and screens. The fascia is steel. Interior partitions are gypsum board on steel studs. All the houses have air conditioning and all-electric equipment.

DEMONSTRATION TOWNHOUSES, Houston, Texas. Owners (sponsors): *American Iron and Steel Institute, Houston Lighting & Power Co., General Electric Co.* Architects: *Wilson, Morris, Crain, & Anderson.* Engineer: *James A. Cummins.* Landscape architect: *Fred Buxton.* Interior designer: *Jack Evans.* Developer: *Dwight M. Nichols, Jr.* Builder: *Sam Johnson.*

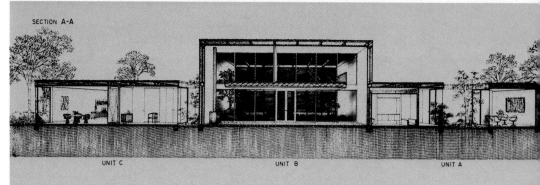

SECTION A-A

UNIT C   UNIT B   UNIT A

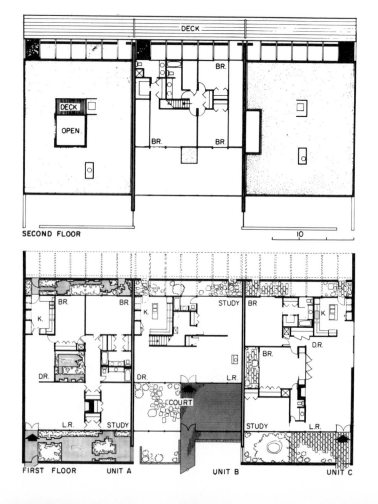

SECOND FLOOR   10

FIRST FLOOR   UNIT A   UNIT B   UNIT C

The two-story central house, (unit B on plans and section) is given an unusually spacious quality by the full-height atrium (right), which is enclosed by operable wood louvers. These louvers—together with the brick floors which continue through the main floor—add a great sense of texture and warmth to the exposed steel beams and built-up angle or "star" columns.

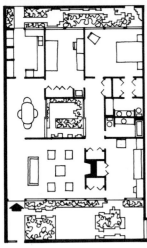

Three courts, at the entrance, center and back, give daylight and a glimpse of the outdoors to most rooms in this house. The living room, dining room and study are all planned for visual privacy, but give a sense of space beyond. Lighting is planned for function and drama as well.

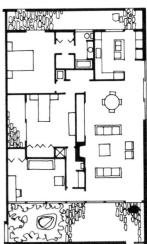

The third house likewise has three courts, and a big living-dining room to gain spaciousness. Most furniture and accessories are steel; most colors are white-gray-beige, with accents of orange and yellow. In varying proportions, these colors form the basic scheme for all three houses.

4 This group of townhouses on Chicago's North Side has an unusually high density for low-rise housing: slightly more than fifty units per acre. Instead of building the 206-unit high-rise that was allowable on the site, the developer, I. Simon and Son, Inc., chose to downzone so that low-rise construction, which was proper for the area, was possible even though land costs became extremely high (about $11,000 per unit). It is to the credit of Booth and Nagle that not only is the street elevation absolutely compatible with the neighboring walkups and townhouses, but the complex has a remarkably open feeling in its courtyards (left). Because of set-back requirements, the dimension across the central space is only 28 feet. But by using two unit plans (shallow and deep), diagonal corners, rounded stair towers and railings in combination with substantial plantings, a pleasant continuous urban mall—which will become more pleasant as plantings mature—has resulted. The A and B duplex units are stacked two high for a total of four floors with a concrete floor separating them.

THE PORTALS, Chicago, Illinois. Architects: *Booth & Nagle.* Engineers: *Wiesinger-Holland, Ltd.* (structural); *Wallace & Migdal, Inc.* (mechanical). Contractor: *I. Simon & Son, Inc.*

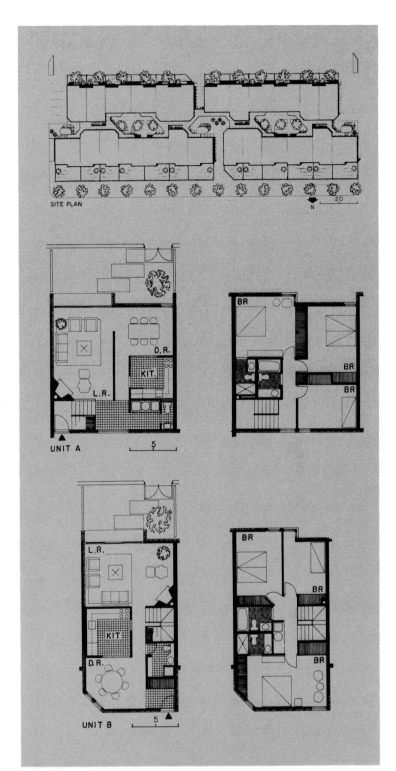

SITE PLAN

N 20

UNIT A 5

UNIT B 5

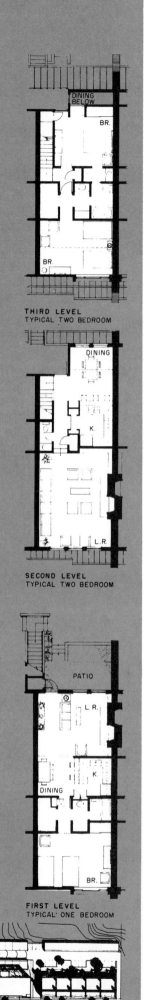

THIRD LEVEL
TYPICAL TWO BEDROOM

SECOND LEVEL
TYPICAL TWO BEDROOM

FIRST LEVEL
TYPICAL ONE BEDROOM

Ray Jacoby photos

5

A simple palette of materials—brick, stucco and standing-seam sheet metal—along with the manipulation of the forms and textures of these materials, creates a good answer to the problem of establishing a peaceful relationship between an existing Tudor building and the new. In the space linking the off-street side of the townhouses to the garages, an auto court was formed. All entrances are from this landscaped auto-pedestrian space. Brick walls divide the structure, emphasizing the scale of the individual townhouse.

Each townhouse contains two apartments (as the section shows). Interior spaces are exciting, especially in the two-bedroom duplex which have two-story spaces with balconies, and garret-type bedrooms with clerestory lighting.

THE ABERDEEN TOWNHOUSES, Oklahoma City, Oklahoma. Owners: *Richard Cain and Jon Cain*. Architects: *Woodward, Cape & Associates*. Contractor: *Ed Hughes Construction Company*.

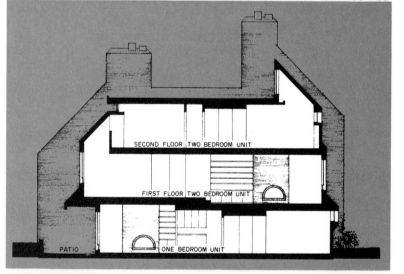

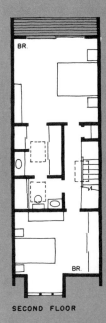

SECOND FLOOR

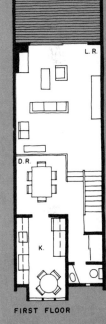

FIRST FLOOR

6 Handsome bay windows form a delightful variation on a time-honored San Francisco theme in these spirited townhouses by architect Jonathan Bulkley. Their trim lines are set off by slanted cedar-shingled roofs, whose low eaves scale the houses, slightly taller and narrower than usual, to dwellings nearby.

By planning them only 15 feet wide, in three stories that run the lot's 40-foot depth, Bulkley provides the dual advantages of economy and privacy for an urban site. Rooms are spacious. An inner, elevated dining balcony varies an ample living space. Sunny bay window alcoves and, behind, tiers of decks overlooking San Francisco Bay extend and brighten well-zoned interiors. The four houses retain a fine humanizing scale.

TOWNHOUSES, San Francisco, California. Owner: *Round Hill Co.* Architect: *Jonathan Bulkley—Takeshi Yamamoto*, associate. Engineer: *Dames & Moore* (site). Contractor: *Askeland & Company.*

Joshua Freiwald photos

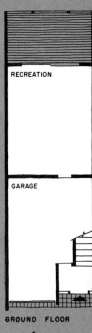

RECREATION

GARAGE

GROUND FLOOR

5

Garden Complexes on Suburban Sites

Garden settings for apartments and townhouses are an old idea in new guise and in greater variety than earlier versions. Usually found in suburban areas or on the fringes of cities where land is less expensive than in town, the garden complexes of today are park-like environments in which are placed various kinds of multi-unit buildings —apartments and "town" houses—offering a variety of living accommodations. Because the site is large, it can be planned with a degree of freedom that permits development of public spaces as more than just circulation, that allows clustering of units and placement of clusters in formal or informal patterns, and in arrangements that assure privacy for the units and their private open spaces.

Indeed, the quality of the site planning in these complexes has become almost—but not completely—as important as that of the internal planning of the units. Quality in both is essential, whatever the market, and it is still of primary importance to build so that noise is not transmitted between units, to use materials which are easily maintained, and to recognize the need for visual privacy between units and the desirability of orienting for sunny patios and balconies.

Density—how many units to put on a site—is an inescapable question, bound by the consideration of investment return as much, if not more than, by environmental quality and attractiveness of the individual units. There is no one answer, however, that satisfactorily works for all sites, conditions, markets, and developers—for density is a relative, not an absolute, term, as the projects in this section on garden complexes well demonstrates. Densities in these projects range from five units to the acre to 18 units per acre, yet it is difficult if not impossible to distinguish offhand which projects are low in density and which are high. The key to a successful project is its site planning and unit design.

Many garden complexes now include a community center or recreation building adjacent to a large pool. In fact, the center is often the landmark for the development, and its distinctive design a positive point in marketing the units.

Garden complexes attract all ages of adults, but especially suit both younger and older childless couples. As these groups grow larger, and single family houses become less available, the economical use of land in the garden complex gives it increasing importance.

1

Water has become a major feature in large-scale housing, for both visual and recreational reasons and for its value in solving difficult site problems. At Sixty-01 near Seattle, problems were serious enough to have prevented use of the land: a one-time hog farm, it consisted largely of peat bogs. Regraded, with the bogs converted to lakes, and the lakes usable for flood control, irrigation and drainage as well as for recreation and enhancement, the site became highly desirable property. But its location in a single-family zone of the city of Redmond, Washington, made it ineligible for multi-family development until the architects for this project suggested—and assisted in drafting—a Planned Unit Development ordinance not unlike that in their own city, Newport Beach, California. Sixty-01 received the first permit under the ordinance. The development was originally conceived by the developer as a garden apartment community, with a density of 10 units per gross acre. This density proved impossible to achieve using only one- and two-story units, without changing the site and losing most of the existing trees. The feasibility of the project was assured, however, by the introduction of a number of four-story multi-family apartment buildings. The siting of these buildings, with their bold uncompromising forms, gives strength to the whole area, and punctuates the rhythmic pattern of the smaller townhouse apartment units. Each of the three lakes is a focus for a section of the project and each section represents a development phase: 351 of the projected 770 units, and the Village Hall (recreation and community center) and the second phase (more of all kinds of units) have been completed; the third phase is a commercial center.

SIXTY-01, Redmond, Washington. Developer: *W-O Company*. Architects: *Riley & Bissell*. Engineers: *Hugh Goldsmith & Associates*. Landscape architects: *John Lantzius & Associates*. Contractor: *North Coast Construction*.

The master plan uses the three man-made lakes as focal points, and breaks the units—townhouse and elevator buildings—into village-sized groups, each with its own kind of unit "mix". The community center relates to the largest lake and the commercial center is located between the two small lakes on a road permitting public use of the shops and restaurants while maintaining the security of Sixty-01 residents.

1. Village Hall & Spa
2. Commercial center
3. Townhouses (2 BR), Bachelor flats
4. Apartments (1 & 2 BR), townhouses (1 & 2 BR), penthouses (1 BR)
5. Townhouses (1 & 2 BR), penthouses (1 BR)
6. Apartments (1 & 2 BR), penthouses (3 BR)
7. Typical townhouse cluster
8. Typical elevator apartments
9. Typical parking garage

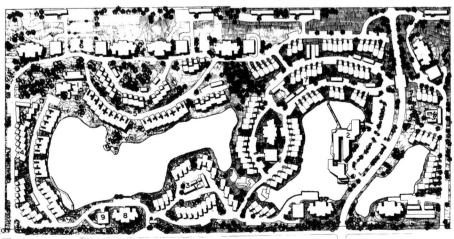

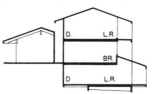

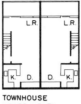

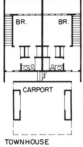

TOWNHOUSE
UPPER LEVEL

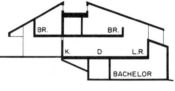

TOWNHOUSE
LOWER LEVEL

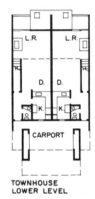

APARTMENT
THIRD LEVEL

BACHELOR
GROUND LEVEL

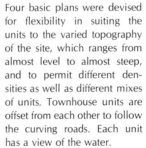

TOWNHOUSE
LOWER LEVEL

TOWNHOUSE
UPPER LEVEL

BACHELOR

Four basic plans were devised for flexibility in suiting the units to the varied topography of the site, which ranges from almost level to almost steep, and to permit different densities as well as different mixes of units. Townhouse units are offset from each other to follow the curving roads. Each unit has a view of the water.

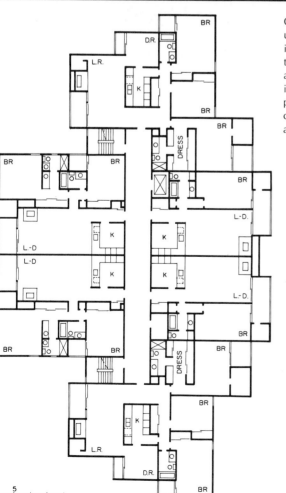

Cedar siding is used on some units, cedar shingles on others, including the four-story elevator apartment buildings and adjoining parking garage buildings. The first phase of the project, now completed, includes 351 units and the recreation facilities.

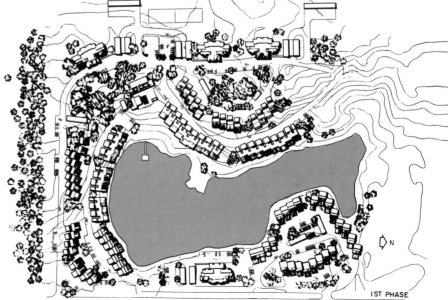

1ST PHASE

Ed Stoecklein photos

2 Working with a construction budget of approximately $12,000 per unit, architects Backen, Arrigoni & Ross have produced this exceptional 296-unit residential community in southern California. The units were designed for rental to young professionals in the age group between 21–35 and recreational facilities appropriate to this group were also provided.

The architects developed the site as a continuous structure (see site plan) out of which a rich variety of outdoor spaces—public and private—were carefully carved. By restricting cars to two peripheral bands, the interior of the site has become an inviting pedestrian network of walkways and courtyards, all beautifully scaled and sympa-

thetically detailed using lighting fixtures, gutters and downspouts, paving and plants. The housing is constructed of conventional wood frame finished in textured stucco and boldly accented in a variety of bright warm colors.

The one- and two-bedroom apartments are functionally laid out and provided with more than the ordinary number of amenities. But the great strength of the design is the richness and variety of its internal spaces. They move in and out, open to invite entry or close to redirect or gently exclude. In some, the feeling of enclosure is forceful. Others are thrown wide open to the sky. All are textured and handsomely planted.

What the architects have also

achieved is a clear sense of community at the village scale. The physical elements are repeated in variations without monotony and they seem to flow together in a united and stimulating composition. This is a place that excites the imagination. This is a place that delights the senses.

———————————————

TUSTIN CONDOMINIUMS, Tustin, California. Owner and developer: *Leadership Housing Corporation*. Architects: *Backen, Arrigoni & Ross*. Structural engineers: *J. S. Papp & Associates*. Landscape architects: *POD-Landscape Architecture*. Interior designer: *Judy Rock*. Contractor: *Leadership Housing Systems, Inc.*

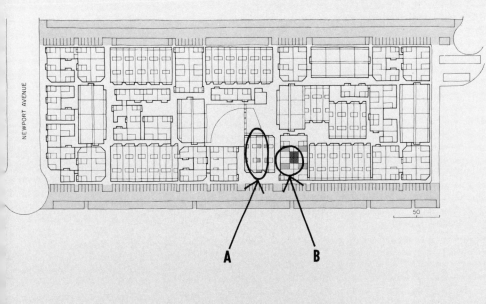

The one-bedroom apartment is a typically efficient urban housing plan with a terrace provided as an additional amenity. The slender, two-bedroom apartment is an interesting variation on the city brownstone plan. Here the living-dining space has been drawn into the center of the house and flanked by private patios that assure continuing daylight.

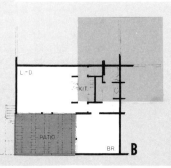

Like the exteriors, the interiors are conceived and executed as simple planar forms in and about which space flows rather freely. The chief finish materials are painted gypsum board on interior partitions and ceilings, vinyl asbestos tile and/or carpeting on floors, ash for wood doors and cabinets and plastic laminate for kitchen counters. Sliding window assemblies are aluminum sash. Interior colors are full-blooded and warm but never overwhelm the interior architecture or get in the way of its easy and interesting spatial flow. All apartment units, especially those with multiple patios, have more than adequate provision for ventilation.

Norman McGrath photos

3

Privacy—and especially private outdoor space—is difficult to achieve at townhouse densities. But architect Hugh Jacobsen has achieved it effectively in his designs for Tidesfall, a 54-unit lakeside community in the new town of Columbia, Maryland. He simply extended the common walls beyond the enclosed space (photo top, opposite) to screen 12-foot-deep decks and, on some units, balconies off the master bedrooms.

Glistening white stucco over block, these wing walls are also, of course, the major design element—giving a hard edge against the sky and creating an ever-changing pattern of shadow and light on both the street side (above) and the view side of the groups of buildings.

Four models were designed by Jacobsen for Page Construction Corporation, the developer. The two-level units range from 1,540 to 2,275 square feet, plus full basement. Three of the four are 22 feet wide, but one model, for use at the end of rows, is 26 feet. The model shown in plan and interior photos (and the center unit in outside view) is a three-bedroom unit. By lowering the living room five steps, Jacobsen gave the space a 12-foot ceiling and created the "balconied" dining room.

In one model, a fourth bedroom (or library) is built above the carport, reached by a bridge across the entry patio between the garage and the house. In another model, a fifth bedroom is created by cutting the master bedroom to 13 by 15 feet.

All units have fireplaces, air conditioning, oak floors, thermal glazing, and make effective use of skylights to brighten middle-of-the plan areas. All utilities (as elsewhere in Columbia) are underground.

TIDESFALL, Columbia, Maryland. Owner: *Page Construction Corporation.* Architect: *Hugh Newell Jacobsen.* Structural engineer: *James Madison Cutts.* Interior design: *Hugh Newell Jacobsen.* Contractor: *Page Construction Company.*

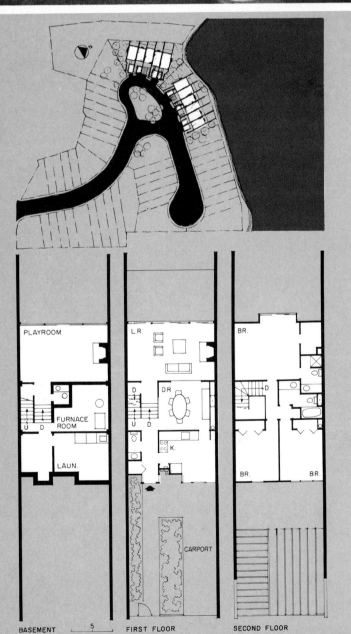

BASEMENT — 5 — FIRST FLOOR — SECOND FLOOR

PLAYROOM · FURNACE ROOM · LAUN. · L.R. · D.R. · K. · BR. · CARPORT

N 25

4 This sprightly community of 282 townhouse apartments for married students is the first phase of Collegetown, a larger proposed development and adjunct to the Sacramento State College campus. The master plan envisions eventual construction of high-rise apartments and garden apartments in a nice mix, and a variety of commercial and community amenities. Although this is just a portion of the larger scheme, it is neatly complete in itself, with a community center, landscaped open spaces and courts, and sunken and heavily landscaped parking areas. There are one-, two-, and three-bedroom apartments in the complex, arranged in clusters around the courts. An amazing variety and vitality has been given the design, even though all but the smallest apartments are variations or combinations of identical 20-by-20-foot-square units. The buildings are wood frame, with cedar siding, drywall interiors and oak floors; each apartment has its own enclosed patio. The architect states that his goal "was to design an exciting, yet stable and self-supporting com-

SECOND FLOOR

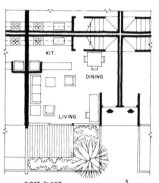

FIRST FLOOR

Except for the one-bedroom one-story units, all apartments are a variation on the identical 20-by-20-foot-square floor plan. Variations are achieved by the addition of a study on the ground floor or a bedroom over an underpass or by raising the unit over a storage area. Added variety is given by different sunshades, depending on the orientation. Each unit has the living area on the entry floor and its own bedrooms above, so no one lives over anyone. A community recreation facility is shown above.

munity." Concerning the development's cost, he adds that, "the economic aim of a self-supporting community for students and faculty, with rents that all can afford, was achieved in phase 1 through FHA 221(d)3 low interest loans, the State College Foundation's tax exemption, and economy in planning and design . . . the low cost of construction was realized by establishment of an efficient floor plan which is repeated . . . and by simple wood frame units which back up to cavity walls that distribute all utilities."

COLLEGETOWN, Phase 1, Sacramento State College, Sacramento, California. Architects: *Neill Smith and Associates; Dreyfuss & Blackford* (supervision). Engineers: *GFDS Engineers* (structural); *Alexander Boome* (mechanical/electrical). Landscape architect: *Lawrence Halprin & Associates.* Contractor: *Nielsen Nickles Company.*

Joshua Freiwald photos

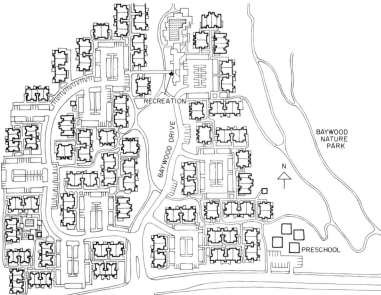

5 Baywood is an apartment and townhouse community in Newport Beach, on the coast of Southern California, developed to offer an amenity in living different from—but as pleasant as—that available in other such projects of the developer, The Irvine Company. Not only is the physical environment designed to provide for middle-income people a lush landscape—replete with plantings of trees which, at maturity, will be tall and leafy and of smaller scale bushes and shrubs—but the site plan innovatively accommodates the various stages of the life cycle. There is, for instance, a section of the development where units are specially for single persons and for adults without children; another, for families of different sizes; and a third for a mix of families and childless adults to whom proximity to children is no problem.

The site lends itself to such a separation of unit types and clusters. Originally a bare hilltop cut by two gullies, the 20.7-acre site has been planted around one of the gullies as a landscaped central mall, winding through the development to its focal point (the clubhouse building) at the north end of the property. Three natural divisions of the topography separate the unit types: one- and two-bedroom apartments for adults (singles and adults with children) are on the west; a mix of two- and three-bedroom apartments and a few townhouses (for families and adults without children) is in the center, set back from but running along the principal section of the mall; and on the east is a mix of two- and three-bedroom apartments and townhouses.

The east section overlooks an unusual amenity—the second gully, left in its natural state as a nature study park for use of all the residents. It is a permanent open space which, along with the topography of the area, buffers Baywood from adjacent developments.

The dominant architectural feature of Baywood is the clocktower of the clubhouse. Not only is it a focus for the community but the clear view of the tower from the freeway is a pleasantly subtle—and economically important—advertisement for the project. Located at the far end of the main road, the clubhouse can only be reached by traversing the length of the central mall, a process which unfolds a series of tantalizing vistas of the community, bound to impress the visitor and delight the resident.

There are 320 units on the site—15 per acre—yet, thanks to the considerate, skillful and imaginative use of the site, there is neither crowding nor loss of individuality.

BAYWOOD, Newport Beach, California. Owners and developers: *The Irvine Company—William Watt, vice president, Multi-Family Housing Division.* Architects: *Fisher-Friedman Associates—Rodney Friedman, partner-in-charge; Robert Geering, project architect.* Engineers: *Leonard F. Robinson & Associates* (structural). Landscape architects: *Sasaki, Walker & Associates.* Contractor: *The Irvine Company.*

The clubhouse, with major recreation both inside (lounges and game rooms) and outside, and administrative offices for the development, is a meeting place for the community. The junior-sized olympic pool, available for use of all residents, is bordered on two sides by two- and three-bedroom units. A secondary, smaller recreation area with pool is located at the southeast corner of the project in the adult section. Carport parking is provided for residents at a number of points, with open parking for visitors.

6 Difficult site conditions were largely responsible for the rugged, idiosyncratic character of this housing in Mill Valley, California. Architects O'Brien and Armstrong began by fitting as many parking spaces as possible on the small level area adjacent to the street. The resulting position of the retaining wall and the existing redwood and bay trees on the steep, wooded portion determined the location of the two structures. There are three apartments in the building atop the wall and one in the house to the right, a total limited by parking space and not by zoning which would have allowed 16 units on the two-acre site. Since there is no view from the hillside, all windows in the larger building look out to the sides. The weathering steel roof and the redwood rough-sawn board and batten siding help the buildings to seem at home among the long lines of the nearby trees.

At night, almost no light can be seen from the street to disturb the darkness of the redwood grove. The one window visible on the highest unit is on the top floor of the house and lights the living room as well. The other three apartments, two of them duplexes, are tucked into the larger of the two buildings.

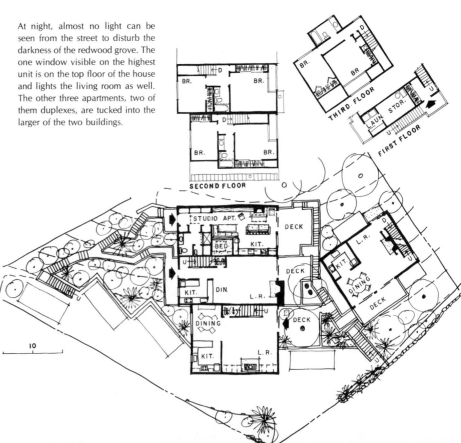

MILL VALLEY APARTMENTS, Mill Valley, California. Owner: *Kal Lines*. Architects: *O'Brien & Armstrong*. Engineers: *Schaff and Jacobs* (structural); *Arthur T. Knutson* (soils). Contractor: *Warren H. Holmes*.

The extraordinary steepness of the site is apparent in the section, in the retaining walls and in the stairways and in the precipitous view looking down onto the decks of the duplex apartments that have been carefully fitted in among the redwoods. One grows through the middle of the deck outside the lowest apartment.

SECTION
5

Philip Molten photos

7

The Carlmont Comstock Apartments are in the luxury class, their design premised on the need of older tenants for living units which approximate a private residence in amenity but which the tenant does not have to maintain. Given these requirements and the two-way slope of the site, a three-story garden apartment proved more suitable than a high-rise building (although this was considered). The entrance to the complex is from the upper side of the site which permits parking in the three-level parking structure along the street. Access to individual units is over landscaped walks, by bridges or by steps which define the variety of spaces and levels. Tenants walk up or down only one flight from the garage. Many of the large oak trees on the site were preserved to enhance the view from each apartment. Privacy between apartments—important in tenant satisfaction—is obtained through separation of balconies, location of windows, and double walls and carpeted floors. Recreation facilities are on a level some 15 feet below adjacent apartment units to reduce noise. Construction is wood frame and stucco.

CARLMONT COMSTOCK APARTMENTS, Belmont, California. Owner: *Edward Drotleff.* Architects: *Knorr Elliott & Associates.* Engineers: *Stefan J. Medwadowski* (structural); *O'Kelley and Schoenlank* (mechanical/electrical). Landscape architects: *Sasaki, Walker Associates, Inc.* Contractor: *H. J. Drotleff & Sons.*

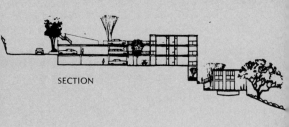

SECTION

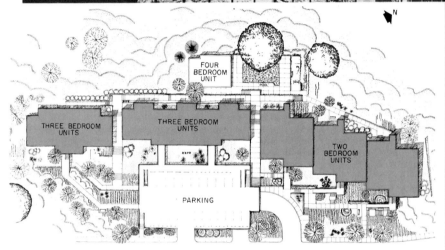

FOUR BEDROOM UNIT

THREE BEDROOM UNITS

THREE BEDROOM UNITS

TWO BEDROOM UNITS

POOL

PARKING

N

20

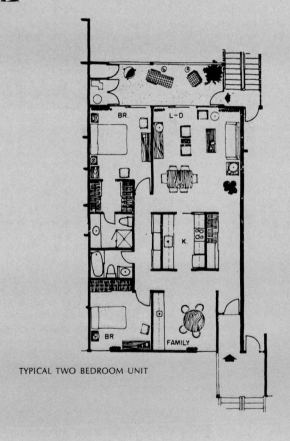

BR.

L-D

K.

BR

FAMILY

TYPICAL TWO BEDROOM UNIT

TYPICAL THREE BEDROOM UNIT

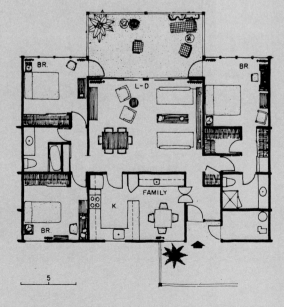

BR.

L-D

BR.

FAMILY

K.

BR.

5

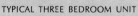

Cedar siding and constant roof pitches (providing units on second floor with high interior space) give pleasing unity to the 114-unit scheme. Typical apartments are clustered back to back, with the clusters in turn grouped to form complex patterns around small commons and more spacious recreation center green. View, left, shows typical entry from parking bay.

8 If providing unity with individuality keynotes the success of a planned apartment scheme, then this California community by architects Fisher Friedman Associates not only succeeds, but incorporates many delightful and original variations on the theme. A major desire, the developers of the complex recognized from the start, was to offer the same feeling of individuality and privacy to every resident that is achieved in a single home, and the architects complied, achieving separate entries for every unit and a great variety of orientations and configurations that were possible within the basic plans. A particularly well-suited example of a community center (a trend that seems implicit in total apartment community design) has been included and made, quite logically and naturally, the nucleus (visually of course, and in a sociological sense as well) of the design. The recreation hall functions well as a focus for the plan, and its central greenway (with whirlpool and swimming pool), the major of several outdoor courts, the unifying element for the many-unit, multi-court design. The greenways permitted nearly every apartment a balcony or patio facing the outdoors (each

SECOND FLOOR

FIRST FLOOR

10

of these is equipped with 10-foot-wide sliding glass doors)—the remaining apartments all having exposure to the south. Outdoor privacy is assured for the complex as a whole by the battlements the apartment walls themselves create, and for each unit by solid patio fencing and balcony rails. For all the spaciousness of the common ground, landscaped by Sasaki-Walker Associates with meandering paths and shade trees, the entire scheme gives the apartment units an average floor space of 1,150 square feet each.

MARINER SQUARE, Newport Beach, California. Owners: *The Irvine Company*. Architects: *Fisher Friedman Associates*. Structural engineer: *L. F. Robinson & Associates*. Landscape architect: *Sasaki-Walker & Associates*. Graphic designer: *John Marsh*. Contractor: *The Irvine Company*.

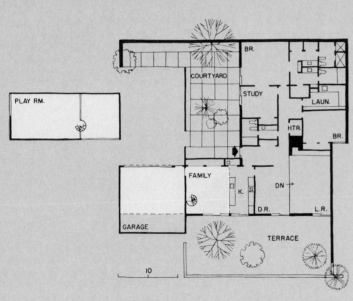

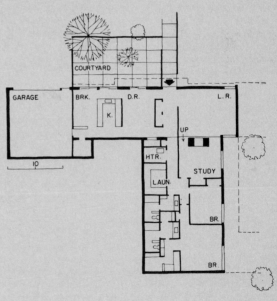

9 Walden is a planned community for 8000 people set in rolling hills southeast of Cleveland in Aurora, Ohio. Its main emphasis is preservation and development of the 1000-acre site's natural beauty. The architect and the developer have a comfortable relationship that grows out of mutually successful accomplishment. No densities are set beforehand. As the architect approaches each new multi-family segment (which are in blocks of ten to each one hundred acres), he works to preserve the natural terrain, and this sets the density for that particular segment. In the first ten-acre area, for instance, a stream and two heavily wooded slopes were the natural features in which 38 units were set. For the buildings, the developer asked that each unit have maximum privacy; that there be no more than three suites per building so that local, not state, codes might govern; and that the buildings not have a multi-family look. All structures are factory-built in wall, floor and roof sections, then field-assembled.

WALDEN Aurora, Ohio. Architects: *Architectural Design Partnership—William B. Morris*, project architect. Civil Engineer: *James Morris.* Contractor-Developer: *Manny Barenholtz.*

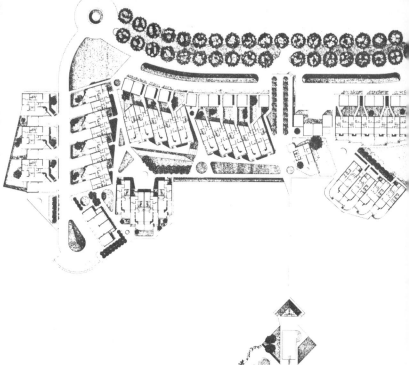

10 There is a rare kind of appropriateness to this cluster of townhouses—built in the early stages of what will be a 500-acre community just outside Albuquerque. Most obviously, the clustering, the use of adobe, and some of the forms are traditional. But where tradition is called on,

it is called on for the way it works and not the way it looks.

The massive adobe walls serve as heat reservoirs—blocking heat during the day and releasing it at night; the walls are essentially blank on the western wall, but open wide on the east (bottom in

plan) to the views down the semi-arid mesa to the contrasting green band along the Rio Grande.

The major glass areas (see photos opposite) are set back beneath deep concrete fascias; and even small windows are set deep in recesses in the walls. To add light

The bold exterior walls of La Luz are stuccoed adobe, and some of the adobes were made on the site from site material. Lintels are sand-blasted concrete; roof framing is wood with six inches of insulation; ceilings are fir; floors are brick or hardwood.

The units shown here are the medium-density section of the planned development of the 500-acre site. 200 acres of the site, including a major piece of the mesa and all of the wooded land along the river will be left untouched.

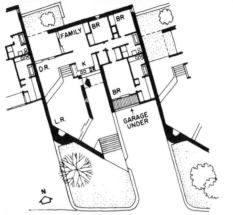

Jerry Goffe photos

without heat or glare, some walls are stuccoed white to bounce light into a room.

Not just the sun, but the wind, is a major factor in the design. High walls protect yards and patios from the wind; but cross ventilation in summer is assured by the placement of the buildings on the slope. In contrast, the often strong and dust-laden spring wind, typically from the west, is blocked by the closed walls of the complex.

And perhaps equally essential, at least psychologically in this dry area, are the fountains in the patio areas.

As the plan above shows, the major living spaces—with their changes of level and wall plane—all open wide to the view and the breeze; the neatly zoned bedroom area is, appropriately, more sheltered. Because of the changes in the site contours, the interior spaces of the units are pleasantly varied.

LA LUZ, Cochiti, New Mexico. Owner: *Ovenwest Corporation.* Architect: *Antoine Predock.* Contractor: *Gunnar Dahlquist.*

11 One of the few architects in the Southwest pursuing regional themes, Antoine Predock has developed a highly flexible housing scheme for Cochiti, New Mexico. His success with La Luz, an earlier project, led Great Western Cities, Inc., developers of Cochiti, a new, recreation-oriented community on leased Indian land, to ask him to design these condominium models.

In order to facilitate his client's sales program, Predock has three basic schemes, each of which can be purchased with varying numbers of bedrooms. Units are designed to be expanded from a central utility core. When more than two bedrooms are desired, a second story is added. All units are 25 feet wide and are separated from the neighbors by continuous masonry walls. The garages, although optional, permit owners to safely store boats when the house is not in use. They also shield the entry courts, providing visitors protection from dust storms and winter winds.

The flat roofs with stuccoed masonry parapets are, of course, derived from Pueblo antecedents but also help to hide the air-conditioning condensers and other mechanical equipment so necessary for desert living. Windows and glass doors are recessed into the masonry wherever possible to reduce cooling loads.

COCHITI TOWNHOUSES, Cochiti, New Mexico. Architect: *Antoine Predock—Stanley G. Moore*, associate. Engineer: *Allison Engineering* (mechanical). Landscape architect: *Sasaki Walker Associates*. Contractor and owner: *Great Western Cities, Inc.*

Two of the available designs have one story with living and dining areas oriented either to the mountain views, left plan, or inward to the court, center plan. The living-dining room and entry court of that model are pictured here.

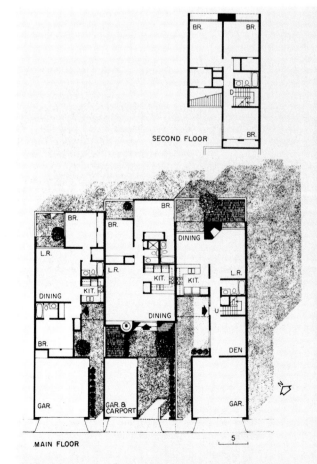

SECOND FLOOR

MAIN FLOOR

Joshua Freiwald

12

Woodside's site is an old walnut orchard in a new and rapidly developing section of Sacramento, California, across the American River from the city's major business area and the state capitol, and adjacent to a state college campus and many new businesses. The plan for Woodside is being developed in three phases; eventually there will be 800 units on the 38-acre site, with an over-all density of 18 units per acre. The first phase, now complete, shows that this rather intense use of the site can create, through cluster planning and sympathetic landscaping, pleasant and generous open spaces between buildings—a key consideration in renting apartments. Although stucco is the predominant material for the residential units, the community facilities (recreation, guest units and laundry) are faced with cedar shingles. Redwood is used as trim, for balcony railings and stair rails and on the apartment units, and panels of cedar shingles tie the residential and community buildings visually. The residential buildings vary in exterior appearance more by size and type of unit than by difference in material. Six basic plans were used to achieve the variation which gives the development its vitality.

WOODSIDE APARTMENTS, Sacramento, California. Owner and developer: *Robert C. Powell.* Architects: *Donald Sandy, Jr., and Associates.* Engineer: *Shapiro and Okino* (structural). Landscape architect: *Anthony Guzzardo.* Interior design: *Jeannette Interiors.* Contractor: *Robert C. Powell.*

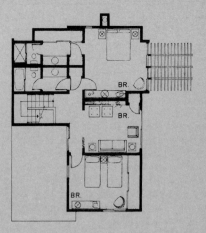

SECOND FLOOR

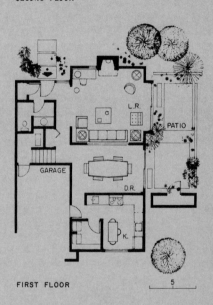

FIRST FLOOR

5

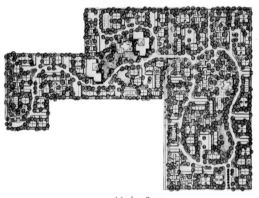

Apartments at Woodside range in size from studio (two types: with balcony bedroom, and all-on-one-floor) to three-bedroom, two-and-a-half-bath units, and rents range accordingly. Each unit has some form of private outdoor space, either a walled court (first floor units) or a deck (second floor units). Some of the more luxurious units are on two levels. Fireplaces —a big selling point with rental agents—are a feature of most apartments. Average age of renters is 37; 62 per cent are young single people who make good use of the recreation units and social center.

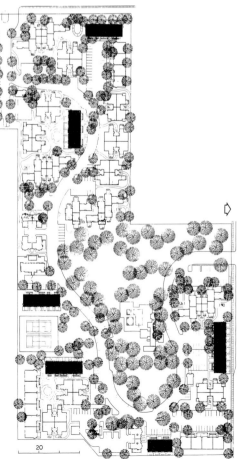

20

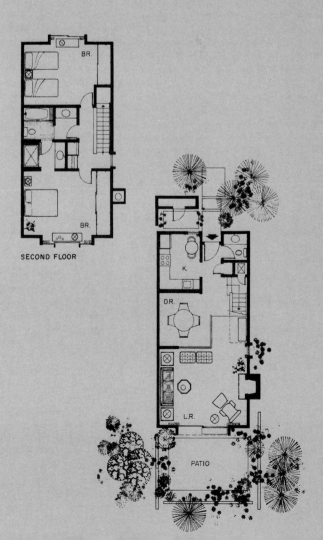

SECOND FLOOR

13

Each of the 125 apartments in this development is part of a "quadplex" module which is designed to adapt to the changing grades of the rolling site and to increase construction efficiency. The modules are arranged in three S- and three U-shaped groups which interrelate buildings and land (within stringent zoning restrictions which limit both building size and configuration), and permit each unit to have some kind of private outdoor space—court, balcony or deck. The three-story buildings contain one- and two-story apartments; two-story buildings have one-story apartments.

OAK HILL ESTATES, Philadelphia, Pennsylvania. Architect: *Louis Sauer Associates.* Engineer: *Joseph Hoffman and Associates* (structural). Plant material consultant: *Joachim Tourbier.* Developer: *E. J. Frankel Enterprises, Inc.*

Otto Baitz photographs

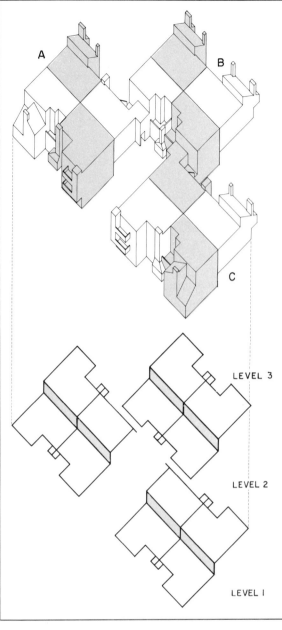

LEVEL 3

LEVEL 2

LEVEL I

14

Wesleyan Hills is an upper-income development of town houses in Middletown, Connecticut, where a very low density (7.26 per acre) was desired. The very slightly rolling site permits a very open and straight-forward use of the 8.81-acre site, with the land sloping on either side of the buildings, and a lightly wooded area on both sides which acts as a buffer between the development and the town. The architect provided the developer with various dwelling unit plans which could be combined in a number of ways. There are 56 two-bedroom units and eight three-bedroom units and a pool for community use. Parking is both under cover and open. Exterior materials vary but were selected for a recognizable relation to each other.

WESLEYAN HILLS, Middletown, Connecticut. Owner: *Hill Development Corporation.* Architect: *Louis Sauer Associates.* Engineer: *Joseph Hoffman and Associates* (structural). Land planner: *Emil Hanslin Associates, Inc.* Contractor: *La Cava Construction Company.*

Otto Baitz photographs

BUILDING A   BUILDING B   BUILDING C   BUILDING D

David Hirsch photos

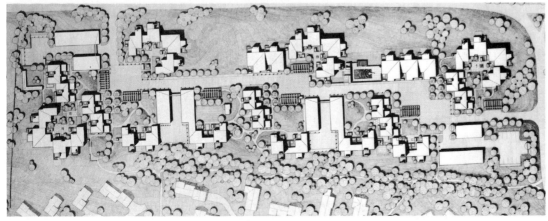

15 Ely Park in Binghamton is a low-rise, no-elevator project of New York State's Urban Development Corporation. Ely Park is suburban; in fact it is outside Binghamton's city limits and water/sewage service had to be provided by an extension from the city (a vital early agreement finally assuring the feasibility of Ely Park). No one walks to work here, and the parking ratio is one to one. Ely Park housing has been judiciously inserted in a beautifully wooded area, on a hilly site that gives some apartments sweeping views of the valley stretching away below.

The Architects Collaborative envisioned this project as a group of single-family residences placed next to each other, row house style, thus keeping the largest portion of the site in common woods, but with each "house" having its own privately fenced front lawn or patio. The houses were to have been erected with modules made in the factory, brought to the site and stacked up quickly. They lost the modular system concept, and the fenced front lawns, between the start of working drawings and the end of construction, but Ely Park still has an idyllic feeling:

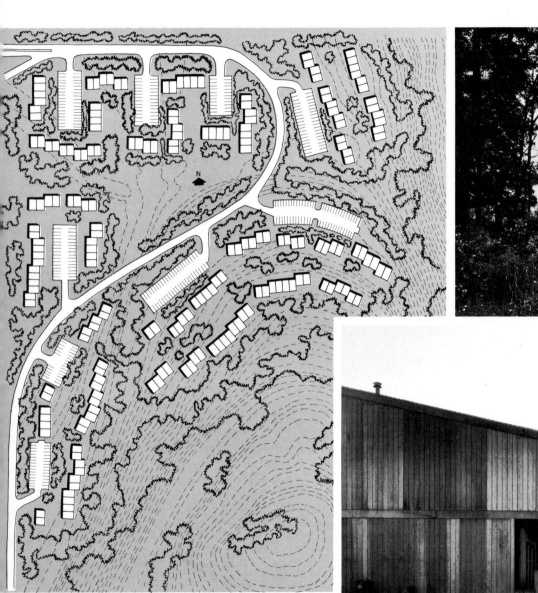

The site plan of Stage I (above) shows how the individual units are clustered near their parking areas, or in line with the contours of the steeply sloping hills. Well less than 50 per cent of the site was suitable for construction because of the slopes, but site work was kept down by careful placement of the buildings. As many trees were saved as was possible, and the area gives the impression of being in deep woods, though it is about a 15-minute drive to the center of Binghamton.

idyllic in the suburban-dream sense of deep woods, wide lawns, rolling hills and a front and back door for the family.

Over 200 units constitute Stage One; 212 units make up Stage Two, identical in construction and site planning. The units are organized in clusters on the site, focusing on each group's parking. Each unit's front door faces a grassy area common to its group of 15 to 30 dwellings. Each unit in the first stage has at least four floor levels and from two to four bedrooms; single-bedroom designs on one level will be included in Stage Two. Construc-

tion was eventually organized in panels, after the idea of modules had to be discarded for reasons of cost and logistics. These panels were made by National Homes, in their nearby plant in Horseheads, New York, using standard 2 by 4 stud construction: the outside skin of plywood, the windows and most of the doors were installed in the factory, then the panels were shipped vertically to the site in large four-sided trucks, and erected. Foundations and all interior finishing and plumbing were prepared conventionally. The plywood siding is vertically grooved with cedar as the

outside layer; the architects detailed carefully to cover all end exposures with cedar boards, as the photos below indicate. This skin has been guaranteed for the life of the buildings and the cedar has been left to weather naturally, with no outside preservative coating.

When you walk inside one of these Ely Park units, you recognize immediately the spaciousness of the dwellings (compared to similar UDC housing or other agency housing) and it is worth knowing how this spaciousness was achieved, limited as these and all other UDC apartments are by tight budget controls.

Wayne Soverns, Jr. photos

If you study the plans and sections of the two-, three- and four-bedroom dwellings it becomes clear that the most prominent additions in space are the "unprogrammed" ones of stairwells, entry vestibules and halls. They are unprogrammed in that agency minimum standards (including the UDC's) do not require them. These transition spaces give real privacy control to individuals within each unit and add both real and psychic "living space" to each dwelling as a whole. The amazing thing is, these plans would be regarded as "inefficient" by many designers: too much gross area given over to halls; so many stairs and landings take away from "living" space; if you eliminated these transition areas you may make the rooms larger, and so forth. But they are anything but wasteful in human terms, and designing efficiently to agency standards is, of course, not the ultimate goal.

When these apartments were designed, the UDC was using room size standards from the FHA's 221(d)3 program, with allowable increases of 10 to 15 per cent. Using those standards as the base, most of the room sizes listed in the plans below meet them, with some significant exceptions. The second bedroom in the two-bedroom unit is substantially larger than the 80 square feet required (plus 10 per cent) as is the living room and the master bedroom in the three-bedroom design, and the living room in the four-bedroom design. These additional square footages probably occurred as much from necessities of the internal geometry in the apartments themselves, as they did from specific design intent; but they are a second part of the reason Ely Park apartments seem so large. The UDC has now developed its own standards for room

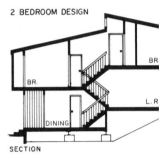

The hallways and upper bedrooms of all units have clerestory lighting, as well as sloped ceilings. There is ample closet space in all floor plans, and three- and four-bedroom designs particularly have almost an extra room in the hall alcove. Some changes have been made in the originally planned services. There are now several large trash enclosures around the site, in place of the individual unit enclosures, and a mailbox island has been located at the entrance to each parking area, as mail is delivered by the rural route carrier.

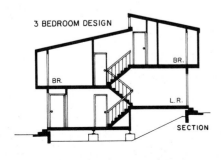

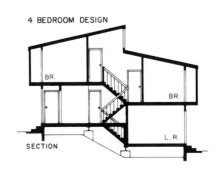

sizes and relationships, and they are always larger than the FHA's 236 program in net areas, though not as large as New York State's Mitchell-Lama program for "middle"-income families (incomes up to $20,000, sometimes more).

The space benefits built into Ely Park did not cost more than UDC's original budget allowed. On the contrary, the TAC project was well within budget, even before the front yard fences were removed. These fences in the two-, three-, and four-bedroom units were never built, as the photographs indicate. Re-moving the fences has opened up the front lawns dramatically, but has reduced the privacy of interior dining areas on the ground floors.

ELY PARK HOUSING, Stage 1, Binghamton, New York. Architects: *The Architects Collaborative—Norman C. Fletcher,* principal-in-charge; *Royston Daley,* associate-in-charge; *Gary Lowe,* job captain; *Robert W. DeWolfe,* landscape. Engineers: *Wiedeman and Brown* (structural); *Joseph Schneider* (mechanical and electrical). Developer and contractor: *Vincent J. Smith, Inc.*

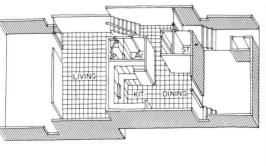

16

Sahalee Village condominiums, located east of Seattle, were designed with three goals in mind: to blend with nature, to achieve maximum views and light while maintaining privacy, and to give each unit an identity for its owner. The key factor in achieving these goals is the slight offsetting of the townhouse units. This offsetting, on a 45 degree line, and placement of units according to the natural topography of the site, channel the line of sight through the natural plant growth and around the buildings to the tall trees. Orientation of townhouse clusters away from each other, and screens on roof and side decks, add to the sense of seclusion.

To preserve the quality of the environment, most of the trees were retained on the heavily wooded site, and the density was restricted to 25 units (two less than the zoning regulation permitted) on the five-acre tract. The offset plan and the exterior vertical cedar siding and red cedar shake roofing blend the buildings with the natural surroundings and make them compatible with the single family residential character of nearby neighborhoods. The existing Sahalee golf and country club, adjacent to the village, is one of the development's attractions and assures additional open space in the vicinity.

While there is a repetition of units, the design solution made individuality possible. Floor plans vary to accommodate one-, two- or three-bedrooms, den or library as well as the more usual spaces. High clerestory and large windows admit the most light possible and open up views to the trees. High, sloping ceilings in all living and dining areas not only give a sense of spaciousness but allow light and air to circulate to the master bedroom and alcove which are on a loft extending over the living and dining rooms.

SAHALEE VILLAGE CONDOMINIUMS, Redmond, Washington. Architects: *Mithun and Associates—J. Donald Bowman,* partner in charge; *James K. M. Cheng,* project designer; *Thomas D. Emerich,* project architect. Contractor: *Swanson-Dean Corporation.*

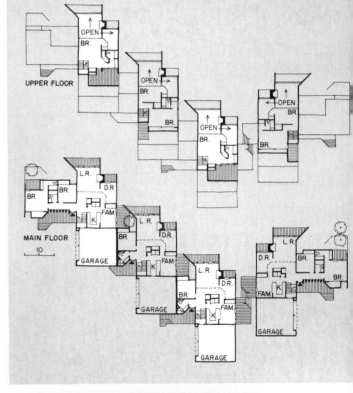

The exceptionally fine site plan, with varied spatial relationships resulting from offsetting of the townhouse units, creates a pleasant visual pattern. Pathways meander throughout the grounds where trees and native plants—salal, Oregon grape, sword ferns—were preserved as much as possible, and where only indigenous plants were added for landscaping. Because of high clerestory windows, views—even from the loft—are opened up. Oak floors and hemlock ceilings in living and dining rooms help relate the townhouse to its surrounding environment.

John Morse photos

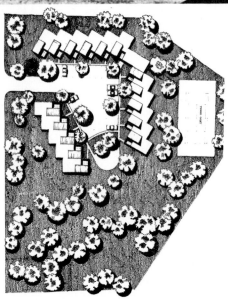

17

On a densely wooded site in East Lyme, Connecticut, architects Rosenfeld, Harvey & Morse designed a 16-unit apartment complex that offers more than the ordinary measure of amenities normally found in the local rental market. Existing trees were carefully preserved and, by emphasizing the natural contours of the site, the architects were able to depress the common parking area to take it out of the direct line of sight from the living spaces. By providing each apartment with a small, partially enclosed patio, then opening the kitchens and living rooms toward the patios, each apartment has an unusual degree of privacy.

Economics dictated the single-story solution as well as the general massing and the level of detail. "Nothing fancy," says partner-in-charge John Harvey in describing the project. "We selected building materials that were in widespread use in the area and therefore readily available. Within this framework we tried to provide privacy and a sense of identification for individual apartments and for the project in general." Tennis courts and a one-bedroom manager's apartment complete the project.

The construction is wood frame, clad in cedar clapboarding and corner boards. Sloped roof areas are covered in asphalt shingle; flat areas are built-up. Interior partitions are finished in dry wall; floors are carpeted. Inside and out, the detailing is uncomplicated and consistent.

The plans are tightly organized and efficiently planned into two-bedroom units, but in spite of their low square-foot areas, these rental units have the design potential for conversion to condominiums at some later date.

INDIAN WOODS APARTMENTS, East Lyme, Connecticut. Owner: *Paul Zazzaro.* Architects, landscape architects, construction managers and coordinators: *Rosenfeld/Harvey/Morse.*

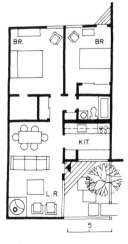

Giraf photos

18

University Park's 200 rental units are located in the heart of New York's Finger Lake region 15 minutes from the Cornell University campus at Ithaca. The apartments, designed to appeal to students and a young adult segment of the population, are one- and two-bedroom units that range in area between 650 and 825 square feet. Each apartment has a private, enclosed patio or balcony.

The prismatic, flat-roofed buildings are staggered to accommodate the terrain and to enliven or individualize a rather dense grouping. Parking areas bite in toward the center of the site at several places (see site plan), but the bulk of the cars are distributed around the site's perimeter—a device that opens the center of the site to a series of pedestrian courts and walks. The staggered clustering of buildings shapes these courts and gives them a pleasant sense of partial enclosure. Located near the center of the scheme are recreational facilities that include a swimming pool, lounge, billiard room, exercise room and saunas.

The buildings are wood frame, clad in scored plywood panels which have been stained white within balcony or patio enclosures and light gray elsewhere. Floors are also of plywood covered with carpet. Street furniture—in the form of built-in benches, railings and light fixtures—enrich the pedestrian way and blend warmly with grass, ground cover and surrounding trees.

UNIVERSITY PARK APARTMENTS, Ithaca, New York. Architects: *Donald Sandy, Jr.* and *James A. Babcock—Diana Crawford,* project architect; *Clark J. Shaughnessy,* production architect. Landscape architects: *Anthony M. Guzzardo & Associates.* Interior design consultants: *Betty Blomberg* (recreation building); *Sagenkahn Design* (apartments). Contractor and owner: *The Questor Group.*

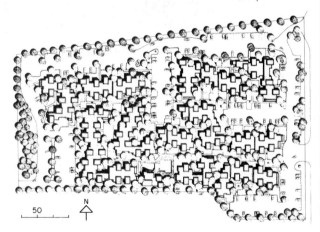

ONE BEDROOM APT.

5

TWO BEDROOM APT.

The game room (photo left) is spanned by wood trusses and brightened by restrained but imaginative supergraphics. In other respects, the design vocabulary is similar in spirit to apartment interiors. The project is designed and executed with an affection for simple spaces and uncomplicated detail.

Designing for Low and Moderate Incomes

Good housing for families of low and moderate income has never been plentiful, and well-designed housing with the kind and degree of amenity that could make for pleasant living has been even more scarce. One reason for this is that subsidy housing—which this has to be—usually is bound by so many limitations and restrictions that it takes almost a miracle to get it built at all. That really good design can be achieved despite such regulations, and that housing which is attractive without being luxurious can be built, is obvious from the broad range of projects, both in type and in location, shown in this section.

The most common location for low-to-moderate income housing is in a city neighborhood, either replacing worn-out buildings or providing new residential buildings in place of other types no longer economical in the area. In such a location, the crucial quality, visually, is the preservation of the neighborhood scale and character, so that the new buildings fit among the existing buildings with a courteous regard for old customs and earlier patterns. That it takes skill and sympathy to accomplish this kind of accord is certain; that

it is not so often achieved is, unfortunately, easy to see.

Happily, however, the sixteen housing groups selected for inclusion here represent the humane and skillful design of deeply concerned architects backed by equally concerned communities and developers. Some of the projects are located in cities, some are on the edges of cities. All of them create a sense of community for the residents, a character derived from the wants and needs of the ultimate users of the buildings. Private open space for each unit is an important a part of the design, as is the quality of public open space; in at least one, public open space is designed as circulation, and is given an engaging character of its own.

A careful analysis of the cost benefit ratio in these projects was a large influence in their design; and the reality of meeting budgets was never out of mind. In meeting the continuing challenge of this field of design and development, these factors assume an undeniable role. For architects, the opportunity in design of housing at this income level looms as large—larger, even—as ever, and their role as perceptive purveyors of environmental quality is undiminished.

1

Canterbury Garden in New Haven, Connecticut, is a 34-unit FHA (236) project on a small city site. Its density is high—21.8 units per acre—and the buildings cover 55.9 per cent of the site; but the plan provides each unit with private outdoor space and gives the project a central public open space as well. Parking is both open and covered, away from the houses. A community room, separate from but central to the townhouses, serves the residents. The plan of the units changed during working drawings as a result of information gained from prospective tenants and provides, in the final design, spaces suitable to the customs and culture of the residents. There are 10 one-bedroom units, eight two-bedroom units, six three-bedroom units and 10 four-bedroom units.

CANTERBURY GARDEN, New Haven, Connecticut. Architect: *Louis Sauer Associates.* Engineers: *Joseph Hoffman and Associates* (structural); *Ceglia Schlein Associates* (mechanical). Planting: *Robert Gregan.* Developer: *New Haven Redevelopment Authority.* Sponsor: *Parish Church of St. Luke.* Contractor: *Kapetan, Inc.*

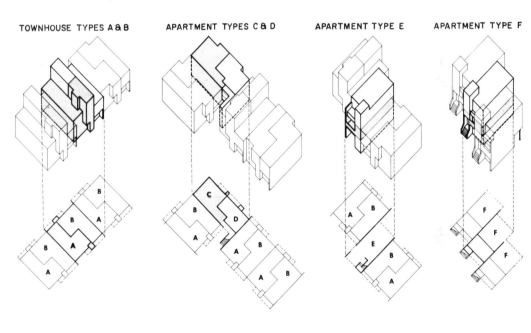

TOWNHOUSE TYPES A & B   APARTMENT TYPES C & D   APARTMENT TYPE E   APARTMENT TYPE F

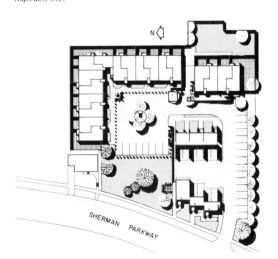

SHERMAN PARKWAY

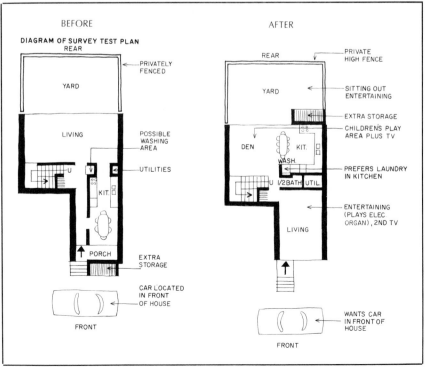

BEFORE   AFTER

DIAGRAM OF SURVEY TEST PLAN

Baltazar Korab photos

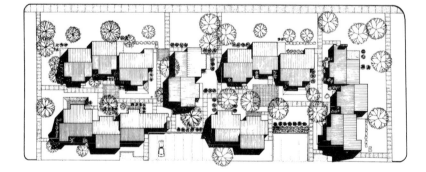

2 This extraordinarily pleasant and well-planned apartment community is a public housing project for the elderly and offers unusual quality for its low cost. The project was developed on three separate sites (the largest one is shown above; the other two are similar to the grouping at the left in the plot plan illustrated) and contain, in all, 36 identical one-bedroom apartments. To qualify, occupants must be over 62, or 55 if disabled. Most of the apartments are built at grade level so the occupants will not have to climb stairs; however, a few units are split-level in arrangement, with apartments one-half flight above or below grade, which enabled more dwellings to be built on the site without destroying the low, domestic scale, and adds considerable variety and visual interest to the groupings. As the three sites border on a major traffic artery,

The informal staggering of units, and the variety of roof heights created by intermingling one- and two-story units gives an attractive, village-like character to this housing project for the elderly. A typical row of apartments is shown here, with adjoining laundry and mechanical rooms; these are arranged in clusters on three neighboring sites to form courts for outdoor living and strolling.

MECH.

LAUN.

K-DINING

BR

L.R.

10

all the units face away from the street and orient toward landscaped courts.

The apartments are well planned and have ample storage space. Several small laundry rooms are scattered through the groupings. Heating is by a hot water radiation system. The buildings are wood-framed and surfaced with cedar shingles. Roofs are asphalt shingles. Interior walls are painted drywall and floors are vinyl asbestos or asphalt tile.

HOUSING FOR ELDERLY, Wayne, Michigan. Owner: *Wayne Housing Commission.* Architects: *William Kessler & Associates, Inc.* Engineer: *William Kessler.* Landscape architects: *Johnson, Johnson & Roy, Inc.* Contractor: *Holtzman and Silverman.*

Jonathan Green photos

3

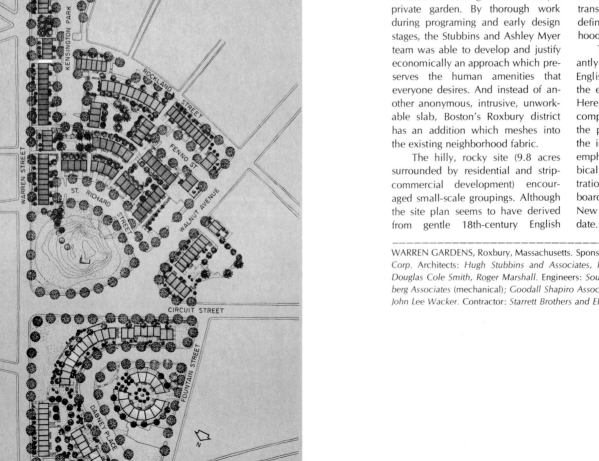

Judicious cost/benefit analysis, say the architects of Warren Gardens (228 low-income housing units), permitted a townhouse—rather than high-rise—scheme which maintains neighborhood scale and gives each family a private garden. By thorough work during programing and early design stages, the Stubbins and Ashley Myer team was able to develop and justify economically an approach which preserves the human amenities that everyone desires. And instead of another anonymous, intrusive, unworkable slab, Boston's Roxbury district has an addition which meshes into the existing neighborhood fabric.

The hilly, rocky site (9.8 acres surrounded by residential and strip-commercial development) encouraged small-scale groupings. Although the site plan seems to have derived from gentle 18th-century English

towns, in practice its geometry is fitted to a site that makes the over-all scheme invisible but provides the pedestrian with a richly varied set of experiences. Passageways between buildings are meaningful architectural transitions and establish a clearly defined scale for the small neighborhood groups.

The houses themselves are pleasantly reminiscent of 18th-century English row houses, too, but never in the endless rows of the mill towns. Here, partly due to the fortuitous complications of the site, but also to the projecting masonry party walls, the individuality of each dwelling is emphasized. The combination of cubical concrete blocks, ordered fenestration and carefully detailed clapboard walls is at once satisfyingly New England and thoroughly up-to-date.

WARREN GARDENS, Roxbury, Massachusetts. Sponsor and owner: *Boston Redevelopment Corp.* Architects: *Hugh Stubbins and Associates, Inc.—Hugh Stubbins, John R. Myer, Douglas Cole Smith, Roger Marshall.* Engineers: *Souza and True* (structural); *Samuel Lesberg Associates* (mechanical); *Goodall Shapiro Associates* (electrical). Landscape architect *John Lee Wacker.* Contractor: *Starrett Brothers and Eken.*

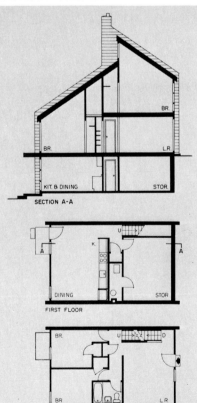

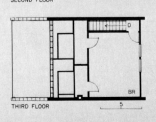

The vast majority of the units have three bedrooms, above, although houses vary from 440 to 1,490 sq ft. This unit is designed to accommodate a substantial change in grade.

4 This handsome low-income housing project is one more complete element in the huge urban renewal area located in Pittsburgh's North Side. This area, which has been under development for over two decades, is separated from downtown Pittsburgh by the Allegheny River.

The site, adjacent to park and playing fields, is owned by Alcoa. Several years ago the company held an architectural competition to design housing for the site. Five developers and their architects competed. The winner, architect Tasso G. Katselas, was sponsored by Action Housing.

From the beginning, Katselas wished to create a tightly integrated village in which private dwelling spaces and public circulation spaces interlock. As precedents

he cites Greek hill towns. He is fond of quoting an old villager in the town of Kastro on Sifnos who, when asked if his house were for sale, replied: "The village is my house."

As the plans and section (overleaf) indicate, Katselas's village consists of 19 apartment blocks containing six apartments each, including one efficiency unit, four three-bedroom units, and one two-bedroom unit. A community building includes additional one-bedroom units. The blocks are linked and entered by open porches at the third-story level and by breezeways at the ground level. Access to the units is by interior pedestrian-only streets or the perimeter parking area.

Such a site plan and apartment block

arrangement is unusual for a low-income housing project but Action Housing was able to obtain approvals from HUD.

The construction is economical and consists of load-bearing masonry walls ranging from three to four stories high combined with precast concrete floor planks and beams. The facing is dark red brick.

ALLEGHENY COMMONS APARTMENTS, Pittsburgh, Pennsylvania. Owner and developer: *Allegheny Commons East Associates*. Architect: *Tasso G. Katselas*. Engineers: *R. M. Gensert* (structural); *Claitman Engineering* (mechanical); *Environment Inc.* (electrical). Landscape architects: *Joseph A. Hajnas and Associates*. Contractor: *Nadco Construction Inc.*

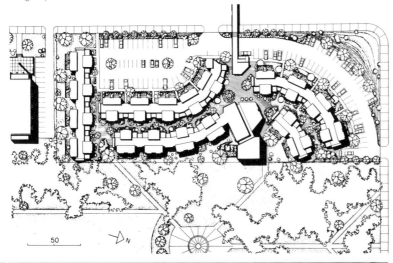

John W. Hobbs

The fenestration of the two blocks shown in the view from the parking lot is revealing of their interior organization. On the ground floor are living rooms with walled patios. Above are the bedrooms of these apartments. The large windows at the third story belong to the living-dining areas of the third floor units, each of which has two bedrooms above on the fourth floor.

Photos by Julius Shulman

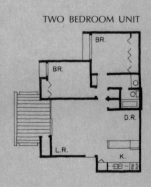

TWO BEDROOM UNIT

THREE BEDROOM UNIT

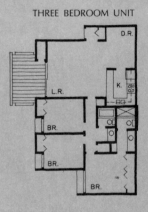

FOUR BEDROOM UNIT

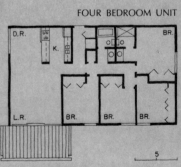

5 To get as much visual interest and variety as possible and at the same time use the available land intensively so that rents could be held at a low level, the architects for the Lord Tennyson Apartments in Hayward, California, near Oakland, alternated large and small buildings, bridged between some of the buildings for vistas, and grouped buildings around landscaped areas developed for community use and recreation. Since this project was built under 221(d)3 regulations, economy was vital. That low-rental housing can be as attractive even if not so luxurious as moderate- and high-rent apartments is obvious from the quality achieved in both buildings and site use in this project. Basic plans, limited in number to effect economical construction, are combined in many different ways to obtain variety. Elevation designs, too, are varied with bays, recesses, extensions of wall planes, and different locations for windows and other "secondary" elements. The common open spaces are pleasant and generous; in addition, each unit has some private open space, with a walled patio or balcony off the living room.

LORD TENNYSON APARTMENTS, Hayward, California. Owner: *Volunteers of America*. Architects: *Stephen G. Oppenheim & Associates—Kurt W. Rheinfurth*, partner in charge of planning; *Harold Wiener*, partner in charge of production. Engineers: *Ralph Goers & Associates* (structural); *Frederick R. Brown* (electrical). Contractor: *Albert Gersten and Associates—Louis Cohen* in charge.

6 This high-density, low-rise housing has been designed so that individual apartments control their own private outdoor space as much as possible. Public spaces have been reduced in size, and the developer is attempting to sell each apartment as a private co-operative. The construction techniques and materials were appropriate for an apprenticeship training program during construction. There is 75 per cent on-site parking, with no parking garages. The Federally-financed 236 project makes sense in its core-city location, attempting to give individual control over property to individual residents. The sponsor was the Labor Assembly for Community Action in San Francisco and the contractor was Maisin-Taylor Associates.

LOREN MILLER HOUSES, Western Addition Redevelopment Area, San Francisco, California. Architects: *Wasserman-Herman Associates— Robert Herman*, partner in charge. Engineers: *Hirsch & Gray* (structural), *Conviser Associates* (mechanical/electrical). Landscape architects: *Baronian & Danielson*. Contractor: *Maisin-Taylor Associates*.

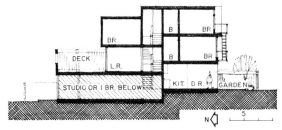

Robert A. Isaacs photos

7 "Unity wedded to diversity" is architect Tasso Katselas' summation of the design approach to this planned new village of apartments and townhouses. The use of similar framing modules, repeated details and standardized component parts gives a consistent element in a complex that has much of the apparent diversity and spatial interest of, say, an Italian hill-town. Katselas's Phase II of East Hills park contains 326 rental apartments and townhouses; sponsorship and the land were provided by AC-TION-Housing, Inc. (through its Development Fund), which is a private, nonprofit civic agency with a basic goal of making available good housing for families of modest income.

Being built in successive phases, East Hills Park will ultimately comprise 1,200 units or more. Phase I (circled red in the plot plan) has been completed for some years and has 187 cluster-planned town-houses and 91 rental apartments.

The apartments in this phase are in clusters of four-story buildings, and the town-houses are cluster-planned.

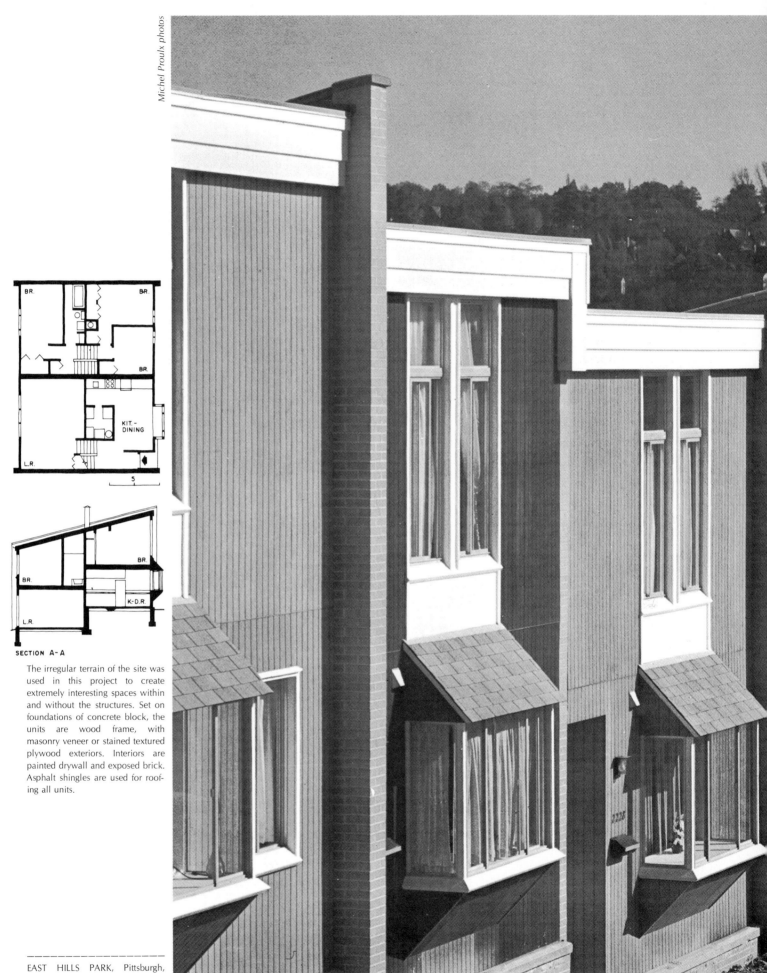

Michel Proulx photos

SECTION A-A

The irregular terrain of the site was used in this project to create extremely interesting spaces within and without the structures. Set on foundations of concrete block, the units are wood frame, with masonry veneer or stained textured plywood exteriors. Interiors are painted drywall and exposed brick. Asphalt shingles are used for roofing all units.

EAST HILLS PARK, Pittsburgh, Pennsylvannia. Owner: *Second East Hills Park, Inc.* Architect: *Tasso G. Katselas.* Engineers: *R. M. Gensert Associates* (structural); *Harold Shratter, Inc.* (mechanical); *Aubrey Caplan* (electrical). Contractor: *The Rubin Development Corporation.*

Jack Stock photos

8 Sheffield Manor, a 36-unit project of the scattered site housing program of the New Haven, Connecticut, Housing Authority, was produced under the HUD Turnkey Program in just 13 months, and was then sold to the Housing Authority, adding to the 3,200 units operated by the Authority. Over half of this housing is low-rent housing.

Tucked onto a narrow but deep one-acre site, Sheffield Manor uses a number of design devices to mitigate the effects of its relatively high density. The two rows of houses overlap only slightly, but even at that point avoid privacy problems because the angled façades aim all windows to the south. To the rear each unit has a yard of its own. The public spaces, including a playground designed by Berman for the almost one hundred children who live there, are designed to be easily cared for. The tenants have maintained a high degree of interest in the appearance of their neighborhood and, according to Sheldon Liner, feel that the design of the buildings is an important

ingredient in determining the quality of their family and community life.

Three types of units have been provided. Twelve of the two-story units (above) are standard two-bedroom row houses. Several are a pair of three-bedroom units combined with an efficiency (plans across page). The third bedroom, in each case, is above the efficiency. Twelve four-bedroom units, three stories high, are also included.

The architect and his partner, Sheldon Liner, were both developers and contractors as well as architects for the project. Sheffield Manor was the first major job for their firm, Structures Incorporated.

SHEFFIELD MANOR, New Haven, Connecticut. Owner: *The New Haven Housing Authority.* Architect: *Alden R. Berman.* Engineers: *Christopher Marx Associates* (structural); *Giordano Associates* (mechanical); *Daniel Gaidosz* (electrical); *Donald Disbrow* (site). Landscape architect: *Donald Biondi* of the New Haven Redevelopment Agency. Contractor and developer: *Northeast Enterprises, Inc.,* a subsidiary of Structures Incorporated.

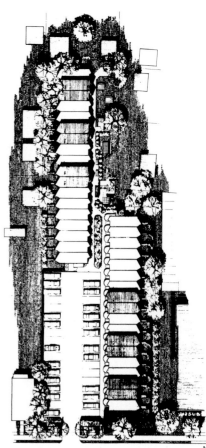

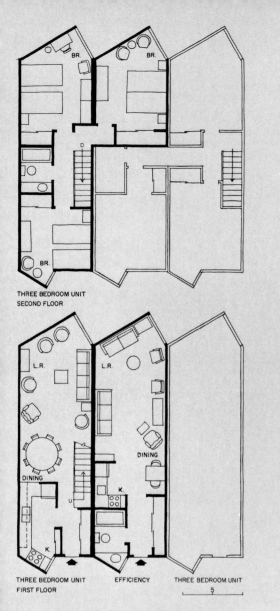

THREE BEDROOM UNIT
SECOND FLOOR

THREE BEDROOM UNIT
FIRST FLOOR

EFFICIENCY

THREE BEDROOM UNIT

5

Where the two rows of houses overlap low site, a change in grade occurs. Striated concrete blocks were laid on the slope to provide an open yet easily maintained space. Unit plans are very similar with only minor variations necessary to add or subtract bedrooms. The three-bedroom units are basically two-bedroom ones which share the floor above an efficiency.

9 Crescent Village, 106 units of 221(d)3 housing in Suisun City, California, by Burger and Coplans, has a number of qualities that distinguish it from public housing in general. First, it is mostly three- and four-bedroom units (except for 18 studio apartments for elderly residents on a nearby site) that are so desperately needed by large families. Second, it makes use of somewhat swampy land that had not previously been built upon. Third, it was extremely inexpensive. Fourth, through the use of bright color and such scale-giving elements as projecting bays on each house, wood fences and tiny entry courts, it seems an

extraordinarily pleasant place to live. Finally, the units themselves are somewhat larger than average. One interesting result of the construction of this project is that Suisun City, which has recently had a marginal economy, now foresees a period of growth, and the architects of Crescent Village have been asked to serve as the town's planners.

CRESCENT VILLAGE, Suisun City, California. Architects: *Burger and Coplans, Inc.* Engineers: *Geoffrey Barrett* (structural); *Tage Hansen* (electrical). Contractor/owner/developer: *Paul Bryan, Jr.*

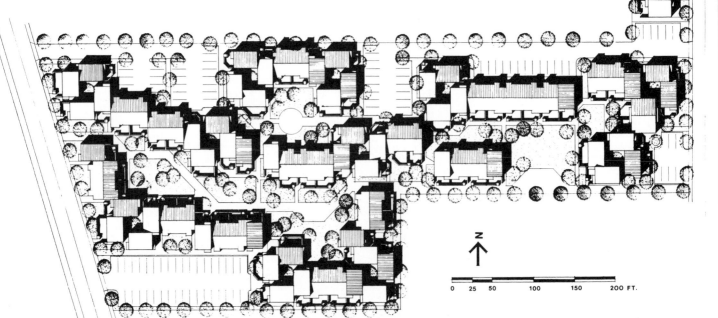

N

0	25	50	100	150	200 FT.

In order to achieve the necessary density of 21 units per acre, the architects developed a side-entry three-bedroom apartment and grouped some of these around entry courts barely twenty feet square. The bright color piece of graphics was designed by the architects.

GROUND FLOOR

0 5 10 20 30 50 FT.

10 The Martin Luther King, Jr. Community, a HUD 221(d)3 project by the Hartford Design Group, is a linear scheme which clearly differentiates between community and private outdoor areas. The architect expresses a relationship of each family's home to the community by emphasizing the approach sequence. Thus, paved streets and courts, with "gates" formed by the buildings themselves lead directly from the city street to his door. These courts, adjacent to the kitchens of each unit, are meant for neighborly socializing and children's play. In contrast, the private areas open off the living rooms and all have grass and trees. The project has 112 units altogether, of which 88 have three or three-and-a-half bedrooms.

MARTIN LUTHER KING,, JR. COMMUNITY, Hartford, Connecticut. Owner: *Van Block Housing Corporation*. Architects: *Hartford Design Group—Tai Soo Kim, Neil R. Taty.* Engineers: *Bounds and Griffes* (structural); *Jacob Koton Associates* (mechanical). Contractor: *Carabetta Enterprises, Inc.*

Upper photos, Tai Soo Kim; lower photo Robert Perron

The neatly detailed concrete and brick bearing wall buildings form open courts in which communal activities are concentrated. On the opposite side pleasant, grassy private spaces have been provided. Each living unit is a duplex with bedrooms above, assuring reasonable cross-ventilation. The recessed entry has built-in rubbish storage, a detail often overlooked in multi-family housing design.

FIRST FLOOR   5   SECOND FLOOR

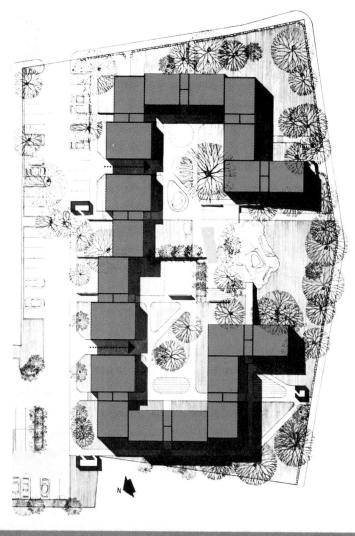

TYPICAL ONE BEDROOM UNIT   TYPICAL TWO BEDROOM UNIT

Phokion Karas photos

11 Trim, modular units, arranged somewhat informally around a central court, are used here with discernment to create an appealing ambience that is all too often lacking in low-cost housing. The site was originally an old estate fallen into ruin, but had magnificent trees and landscaping. Westminster Court in Roxbury contains 70 apartments composed of one- and two-bedroom units. It was built under the FHA 221(d)3 Program.

WESTMINSTER COURT, Roxbury, Massachusetts. Owner: *Development Corporation of America.* Architect: *Carl Koch & Associates— John L. Cummings, Gardner Ertman, Leon Lipshultz,* associates on job. Engineers: *Sepp Firnkas* (structural); *Francis Associates, Inc.* (mechanical). Contractor: *Development Corporation of America.*

Within the neat, disciplined framework of precast concrete bearing walls and floor planks, Koch has used contrasting exterior panels of brick, exposed aggregate concrete and aluminum. The interiors have walls of painted concrete or plaster board. Precast concrete plank flooring is surfaced with vinyl asbestos or oak parquet. Heating is from a central plant, which supplies forced hot water to fin tube radiators.

Given the rigorous requirements of designing 24 low-income units, to be built at absolute minimum cost on a nearly unbuildable site, architects Martin/Soderstrom/Matteson managed a solution that not only fulfills the program, but also provides tenants with the privacy, rich environment and spatial experiences associated with high income developments.

The architects feel the program's innate complexity actually helped create the solution. The site itself is divided by a creek that occasionally reaches serious flood stage. The northwest corner of the property is in a sizable swamp and the north end of the site is bisected by a 10-foot city sewer easement. To further complicate the project, the only access into the property is from a high speed arterial bordering the site on the south. Combined with rigid parking requirements, the program was an extremely difficult one to follow.

Due to the complexity of the site— and economic constraints—it was decided to work with basic rectangular spaces faced with a "false front" defining intermediate inside-outside spaces and to connect the entire development with elevated boardwalks.

Interior partitions are at a minimum, preventing the closed feeling so common to small apartments. Surfaces are treated in strong colors, relating to the exterior treatment which gives the whole project a relaxed, almost "tongue-in-cheek" character. This produces an atmosphere that is playful and easy, further enhanced by the use of stenciled graphics to identify apartments and mail boxes.

RALEIGH BOARDWALK APARTMENTS, Portland, Oregon. Owner: *Associated Enterprises.* Architects: *Martin/Soderstrom/Matteson*—project architect: *Robert L. Foote, Jr.* Engineers: *MacKenzie Engineering* (structural); *Long-Maxwell* (mechanical). Landscape architect: *Michael Parker.* Interior designers: *Will Martin and Robert Foote, Jr.* Contractor: *Cason & West Contractors.*

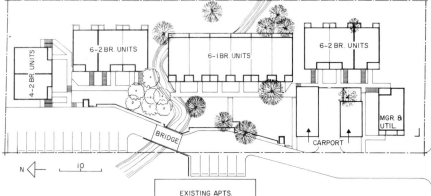

TWO BEDROOM APT.   ONE BEDROOM APT.

5

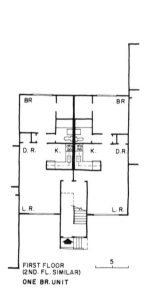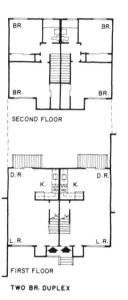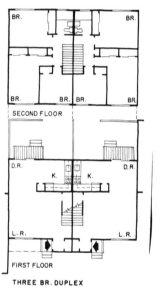

FIRST FLOOR
(2ND. FL. SIMILAR)
ONE BR. UNIT

SECOND FLOOR

FIRST FLOOR
TWO BR. DUPLEX

SECOND FLOOR

FIRST FLOOR
THREE BR. DUPLEX

13 Village Park in Amherst, Massachusetts, is an uncommonly handsome solution to a common problem in small university towns which have experienced enormous growth in the last few years. It is housing financed under FHA 236 and owned by Interfaith (a nonprofit corporation) of Amherst and Development Corporation of America, Boston. The architects placed the 200 units of the first phase on an existing meadow at the west end of the 42-acre site. Another 200 units will be built at the east end, preserving a large woods in the center. Only ten of the units in the first phase have three bedrooms because the FHA was unsure of their acceptance in an untried market. Now they are sure there will be a much higher proportion of them in the second group. A pedestrian street connects all the units and is designed to take advantage of good views to the west.

VILLAGE PARK, Amherst, Massachusetts. Owner: *Interfaith of America* and *Development Corporation of America.* Architects: *Stull Associates—John Olsen,* project manager. Engineers: *Souza & True* (structural); *Lesburg Associates* (mechanical); *Goodall Shapiro Associates* (electrical). Landscape architects: *Shurcliff Merrill & Footit.* Contractor: *Daniel O'Connell's Sons, Inc.*

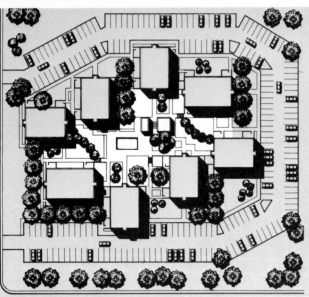

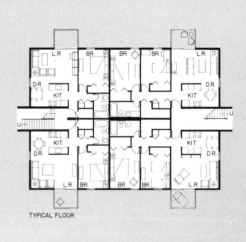

TYPICAL FLOOR

Neil Reynolds p.

14 FHA-insured housing projects are bedeviled by so many economic and technical constraints that it often seems sufficient to praise them for getting built at all. The architects of this apartment complex are understandably proud of the fact that they have been able to build 96 units (half of them with one bedroom, half with two) within FHA 221(d)4 guidelines and with extraordinary economy. They are rightly proud, too, of the individual and social amenities that they have been able to include.

One side of the site for the apartments is adjacent to open farmland, though partially separated from it by a row of mature trees, which fortunately were able to be saved. On the other sides it borders on a neighborhood of single-family houses, and the architects were anxious to maintain their scale.

Accordingly, the façades of the three-story buildings are broken up by changes in material and by patios and balconies that, like the details of the neighboring houses, suggest the ways that people really live. Also in a gesture of good neighborliness the parking lot and its sea of cars was depressed below the existing grade level.

The first two stories of each building are made of precast concrete sections—readily available in the area. The third floors are all of conventional wood framing. Though it was necessary to have many apartments in each building, the architects managed to avoid any sense of claustrophobia or dangerously enforced community by dividing the buildings down the middle and by making entryways, either at grade or by open stairways.

At first glance these apartments make only a modest impression. The architects clearly had their minds on the budget, but they also had their hearts in the right place, for, on closer inspection, this looks like a good place to live—and by all reports is so—within constraints that often are not met effectively.

GREELEY WEST APARTMENTS, Greeley, Colorado. Owner: *The Franklin Corporation.* Architects: *Roark Associates.* Engineers: *Johnson Voiland-Archuleta and Sol Flax Associates.* Contractor: *City Builders, Inc.*

The eight buildings which make up this apartment complex are placed within a peripheral parking area, and they surround a central open space, a place for relaxation and recreation, which for many months of the year in these climes includes swimming. The open space is slightly elevated in order both to shield it from the parking places and to provide a view of the Rocky Mountains in the distance. Balconies and patios open onto the central area and give the occupants of each apartment the chance to survey the passing pedestrian scene.

Robert C. Lautman photos

15 Winner of a design competition for these two city blocks (then in a severe state of blight) held by the Baltimore Urban Renewal Authority, Hugh Jacobsen has created an extremely pleasant neighborhood of contemporary houses which have overtones of Baltimore traditions: flat-front dark brick, vertical windows and small front steps. There are five different house types in the complex—three typical plans are shown here.

The required off-street parking was provided around three sides of the site's periphery. with the center of the land devoted to a common park. Each house has a private walled garden facing the park.

BOLTON SQUARE, Baltimore, Maryland. Owner: *Stanley I. Panitz.* Architect: *Hugh Newell Jacobsen.* Engineer: *James Salmer.* Contractor: *Ames-Ennis Inc.*

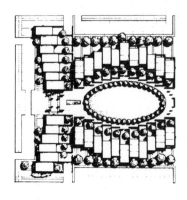

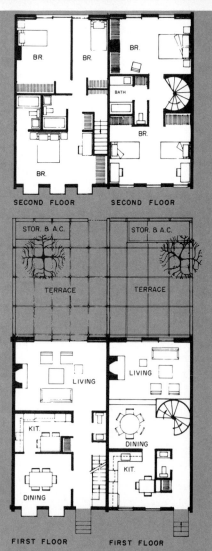

SECOND FLOOR   SECOND FLOOR

STOR. & A.C.   STOR. & A.C.

TERRACE   TERRACE

LIVING   LIVING

KIT.   DINING

DINING   KIT.

FIRST FLOOR   FIRST FLOOR

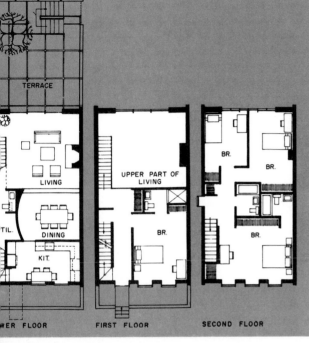

The materials used in the houses are as handsome as the design: the brick is a dark burgundy in color, the mortar a dark gray, the roofs are slate and all of the trim and doors are painted black. The structures are wood frame; interiors have dry wall surfaces. Wide sliding glass doors open each house to its private terrace.

Gorchev and Gorchev photos

16 The buildings of this housing complex in a town near Boston were not chosen for this book to represent a new or innovative approach to housing. Rather, to show a common approach extremely well done. Working within the limits and budget restrictions of the FHA 236 program for low- and moderate-income housing, the architects have produced a group of carefully detailed structures that relate sympathetically to the landscape.

Utilizing the rich potential of the site, the units were turned inward toward small courtyards in which existing topography and large evergreens and hardwood trees were retained wherever possible. Indeed, even during the excavations, adjustments were made to preserve trees and boulders.

The buildings themselves are three-story wood frame structures with cedar siding stained a rich reddish-brown color. Openings for the aluminum window units with insulating glass are trimmed with 1 by 4 redwood boards perpendicular to the building face. These were stained dark brown and give a precision to the façades that belies their simple construction. A lattice along the first floor of the units as they face into the small courtyards gives an appropriate scale.

The interior arrangements place two- and three-bedroom flats on the first floor. Duplex apartments are above with bedrooms on the third floor. Each unit has its own entrance from the courtyard and the first floor apartments have a door to grade from the dining room.

"While designing this project," says Robert Brannen, "we lived with the conviction that a humane, civilized environment must be possible within the constraints imposed by subsidized housing budgets and standards. A knowledgeable, well-intentioned client, a public agency (Massachusetts Housing Finance Association) which never 'looked the other way,' and a design team willing to spend the time required were the combination that did the job."

PINE GROVE TOWNHOUSES, near Boston, Massachusetts. Architects: *The Office of Samuel Paul.* Consulting architects: *Pietro Belluschi* and *Jung/Brannen Associates, Inc.* Engineers: *Benjamin H. Silberstein* (mechanical); *Goodall Shapiro* (electrical); *Homer K. Dodge Associates* (site). Landscape architect: *Joseph Gangemi.* Landscape consultant: *Carol R. Johnson and Associates.* Developer-Builder: *Beacon Construction Co., Inc.*

Three-story wood frame buildings are arranged around courtyards gently set into the rugged New England landscape. Each courtyard pleasantly acts as a small neighborhood for small-scale interaction and opens in turn to the "village common," larger play areas and a community center using three existing older houses. The complex includes a large swimming pool, a child-care facility and an adult activities building. It serves 404 units which have an average density of 25 units per acre.

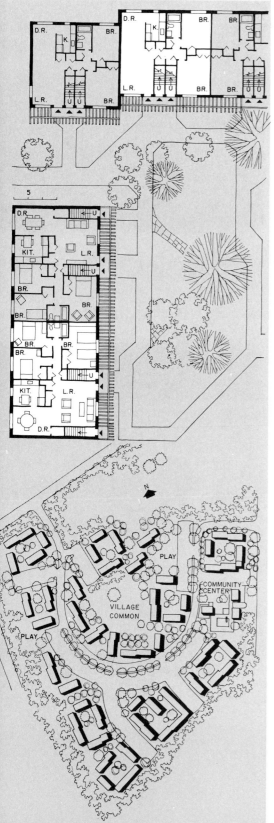

17

Designed to attract—and meet—the rental needs of young families, this apartment group, located in a grove of Douglas fir trees northeast of Seattle, makes much of the open spaces between buildings. For the most part, buildings are clustered around small open spaces containing either play areas for little children or a small number of parking spaces. Very little grading was done to the site since steps, decks and bridges were used where needed to make walking easy on the sloping site. Circulation through the site is carefully controlled, with no through roads. Despite the high density of site use (18 units per acre) there is an unusual feeling of openness throughout, and this is increased in those units which have a view over Lake Sammamish. Other units look out on small landscaped areas. Just three unit plans were used to minimize costs and still obtain variety visually and in rental offerings. Size of units varies from one to two bedrooms. Wood is used for its suitability and because it was inexpensive (at the time of construction), an important consideration in keeping rents low. Rough sawn cedar siding, stained, is used for exteriors, with cedar shingle roofs.

LAKERIDGE VIEW APARTMENTS, Bellevue, Washington. Owner: *Environmental Properties, Inc.* Architects: *Zaik/Miller.* Landscape architect: *William Teufel.* Contractor: *Environmental Properties, Inc.*

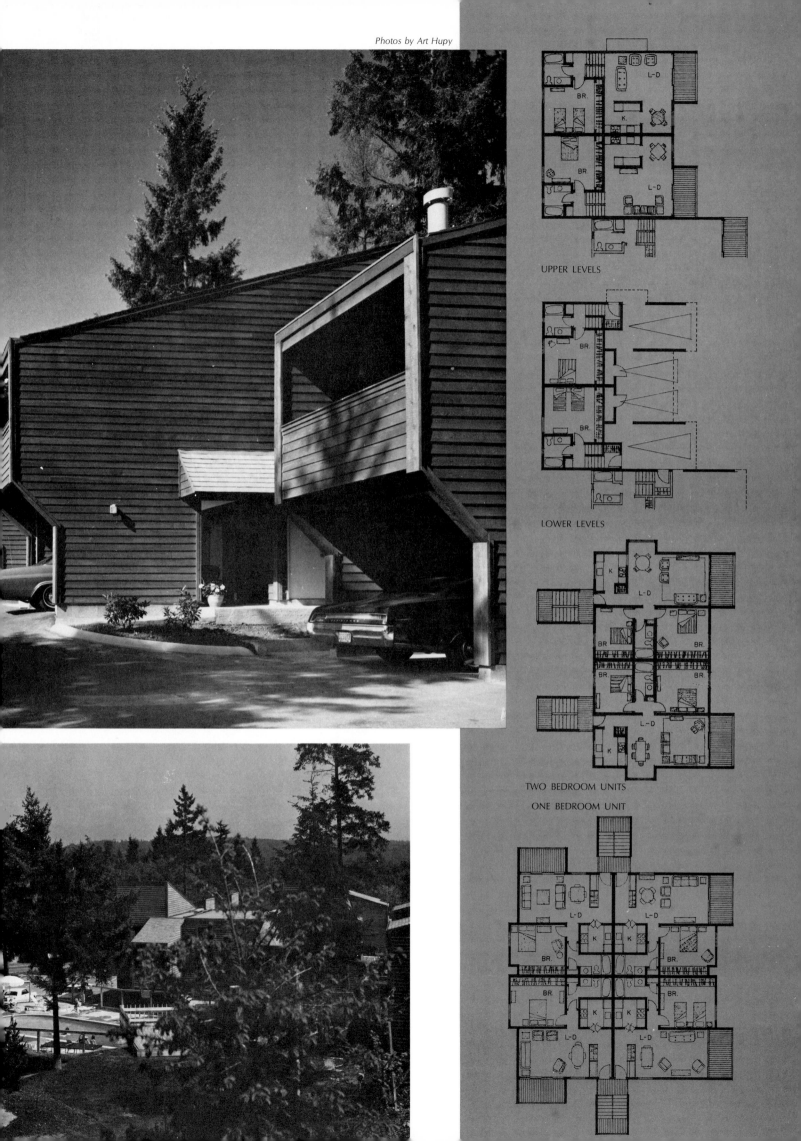

Photos by Art Hupy

UPPER LEVELS

LOWER LEVELS

TWO BEDROOM UNITS

ONE BEDROOM UNIT

18

Friendship Village is the third in a series of remarkably successful housing complexes recently built in San Francisco's Western Addition. And in each case, good design—and each one has been handsome—has grown out of the commitment to quality housing by the late M. Justin Herman and the San Francisco Redevelopment Agency, the selection of concerned young architects and the effort to provide a continuity of community spirit in the new work.

In the case of Friendship Village, sponsored by the First Friendship Baptist Church, 90 per cent of those who moved into the 158 units last June were from the Western Addition area originally. Many of the families are receiving substantial rent supplements so that some four-bedroom apartments rent for less than $60 per month. Thus, it is a shamefully rare example, in terms of most American urban renewal, of well-designed housing for those who most need it in the neighborhood where they formerly lived.

Architects Bulkley and Sazevich worked to maximize the family living qualities of the project, within the apartment, in the design of community facilities, and in the way the buildings relate to the neighborhood. Every unit is oriented outward and the continuous three-story shingled structures preserve the patterns of old San Francisco street fronts. Play space for small children, in turn, is sheltered from traffic. Parking lots are designed to provide playspace during the day and to keep cars under observation at night. In contrast to the rectilinear geometry of the housing, a fanciful, polygonal community building is located near the center of the complex.

FRIENDSHIP VILLAGE, San Francisco, California. Owner: *First Friendship Institutional Baptist Church*. Architects: *Jonathan Bulkley* and *Igor Sazevich*. Engineers: *Jordan and Mathis* (structural); *Harding Miller Lawson and Associates* (foundations). Housing consultants: *Walter C. Lampe and Associates*. Contractor: *Williams and Burrows*.

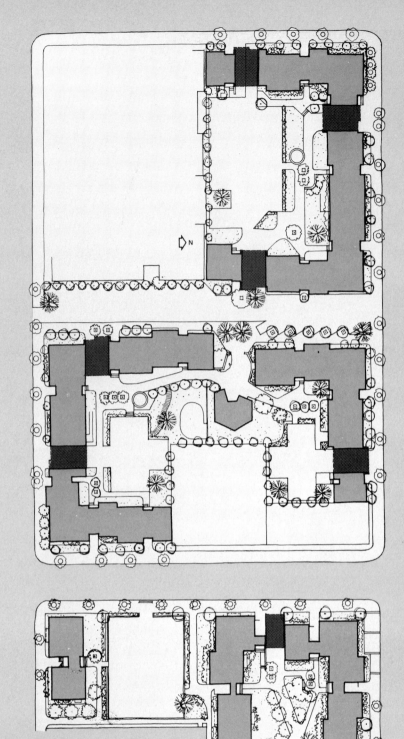

Phase Two of Friendship Village, upper portion of the site plan, was built with less articulation between units than Phase One. Both preserve continuity of the street facade by putting some units over arcades which lead to the interior play spaces (left). The anodized aluminum sliding windows are set in projecting, stained wood frames.

Joshua Freiwald photos

FOUR BEDROOM

THREE BEDROOM

TWO BEDROOM

ONE BEDROOM

STUDIO 5

Five apartment types, ranging from studios to four-bedroom units, have been provided. All have through ventilation and exposure both to the play space and to the street. The community facilities building is unusual, playfully polygonal in contrast to the other buildings. Another playful addition is the front and rear façade saved from an old San Francisco firehouse. The necessary fire escapes, applied in a straightforward way, also echo older neighborhoods.

Conversions

Old buildings with a new life give a city vitality, preserve a scale much more related to human beings than is possible in today's large high-rise buildings, and remind the city of its history. Aside from offering romantic possibilities for unusual kinds of spaces and apartments, buildings which are candidates for conversion from, say, warehouses to apartments, must have both structural feasibility and economic potential: the location must be good for their future use, and the cost of meeting codes and adding plumbing and wiring must be related to the over-all financial return that the converted building can bring in. There are many successful conversions of warehouses to commercial uses, as witness the Jackson Square area of San Francisco, Larimer Square in Denver, Pioneer Square in Seattle, and many individual buildings. Conversion to residential use is more complex but, as the buildings in this section show, can be rewarding in providing distinctive dwelling places and can become profitable as investments and as civic-minded preservation. The successfully converted Prince Building on Boston's waterfront was once a macaroni factory; Westbeth in New York City, now a complex of apartment studios for artists, was a laboratory building for the telephone company. The spaciousness of these old buildings, so desirable and now so unusual, could not have been built today. Preserving the buildings and converting them for much needed housing not only retains something of the city's past, but makes a good and out-of-the-ordinary place for living.

1 Part of the extensive face lifting currently in process for Boston's harbor, this development is fast becoming a highly desirable and effective neighborhood for cars, boats *and* people. The first stage of the project, shown on this page, was the conversion of an old macaroni factory into 32 apartments of one to four bedrooms. Parking for 32 cars is provided on the first two levels. A skip-stop elevator serves the parking levels, and the third, fifth, eighth and penthouse floors.

Later phases of the project include conversion of the dock warehouses into apartments, and construction of the lively townhouses.

THE PRINCE BUILDING, Boston, Massachusetts. Owner: *Trident Realty Trust.* Architect: *J. Timothy Anderson & Associates, Inc.* Engineers: *Simpson Gumpertz & Heger, Inc.* (structural); *Francis Associates* (mechanical). Contractor: *Gerry & Northup Company.*

Richard Graber photos

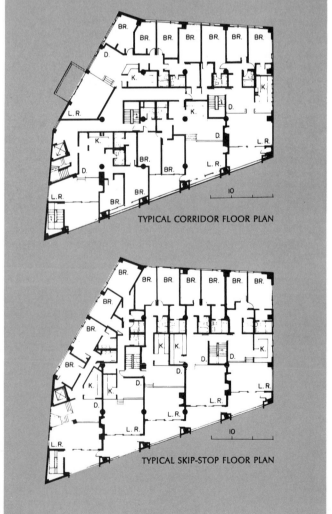

TYPICAL CORRIDOR FLOOR PLAN

TYPICAL SKIP-STOP FLOOR PLAN

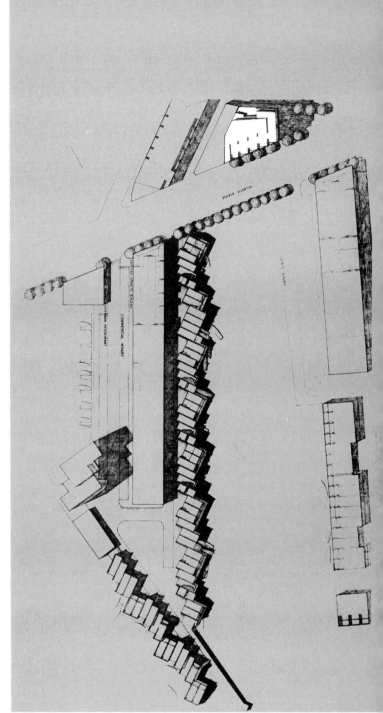

One of the generating design ideas of the Boston Downtown Waterfront-Faneuil Hall Urban Renewal Program is to retain the grand old granite-faced warehouses that for so long symbolized the prosperity of the Boston mercantile shipping industry. This development provides for the preservation of several of these structures, converted into apartments, flanked by a series of varied and handsome townhouses.

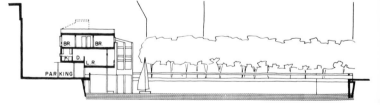

2

Westbeth Artists Housing is one of the few recent projects to provide additional housing units in New York City, and one of the largest and most complex rehabilitation projects in the country. Westbeth can be called a generative experiment in both the financing and physical reclamation problems which occur in rehabilitating an existing structure for residential use. Designed by Richard Meier, the renovation has turned a square block of old buildings in Greenwich Village (formerly used as laboratories and warehouses) into some 384 new apartments for working artists and their families. Painters and sculptors are eligible to live there, as well as photographers, dancers, composers, actors, musicians, singers, writers and, yes, architects too.

Before the present site in Greenwich Village became available, the J. D. Kaplan Fund and the National Council on the Arts had been searching for several years for the proper buildings to house a large-scale living and working complex for artists. They recognized that a growing problem among New York artists was trying to maintain both living quarters and a studio; increasingly higher rents make such arrangements impossible for all but the established artists. After locating the present site, both the National Council and the Kaplan Fund provided interim financing and seed money grants of $750,000 to begin Westbeth as a nonprofit venture. The project is ultimately being financed under the Federal 221(d)3 middle income housing program—total cost of land acquisition and renovation is about $10 million.

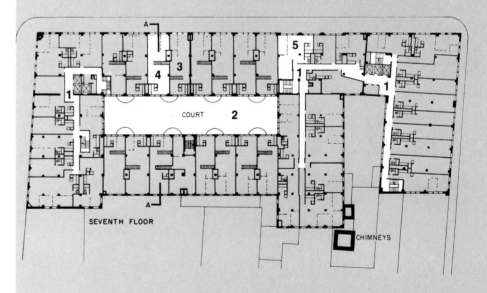

SEVENTH FLOOR

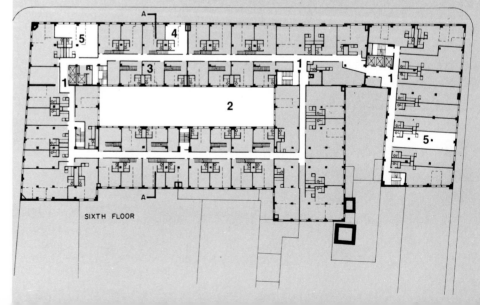

SIXTH FLOOR

SECTION A-A

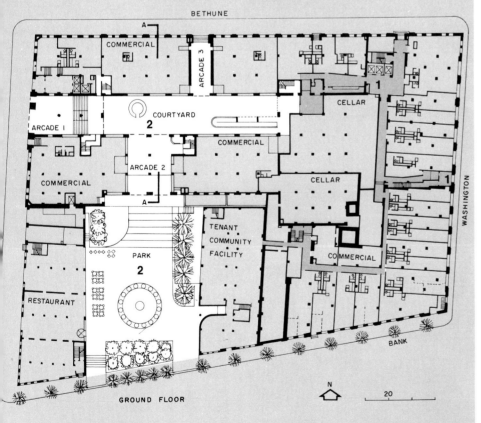

BETHUNE

COMMERCIAL

ARCADE 3

CELLAR

ARCADE 1

COURTYARD

2

COMMERCIAL

ARCADE 2

CELLAR

COMMERCIAL

COMMERCIAL

1

TENANT
COMMUNITY
FACILITY

PARK

2

COMMERCIAL

RESTAURANT

WASHINGTON

BANK

GROUND FLOOR

N

20

1 INTERIOR CIRCULATION

2 EXTERIOR GALLERIES & COURTS

3 TYPICAL TWO BEDROOM DUPLEX

4 TYPICAL THREE BEDROOM DUPLEX

5 TYPICAL EFFICIENCY, ONE & TWO
BEDROOM FLATS

In this photograph of New York City's old Bell Telephone facilities, the façade shown here faces south and Bank Street, while the elevation drawing faces west. (The two central large chimneys in the photograph correspond to the twin chimneys shown in heavy black on the three floor plans at left.) The ground floor plan shows a bank of apartments along Washington Street, but a large portion of its area is taken up by spaces for small commercial shops, a large restaurant, a community hall, and the on-site park. The courtyard is linked to the park by an arcade at ground level, and has a new circulation ramp within it leading to the second floor. Floor plan six is one of the three floors on which a complete corridor loop occurs around the center portion of the complex. The two apartments with their entry floors shown shaded on the 6th-floor plan are connected by stairs to their larger "floor through" second levels—on 5th and 7th floors. In neither case is the "floor through" level directly above or below the entry—rather the stairs lead to the adjacent "module." The apartments shown shaded on these pages correspond to detailed plans. The section above shows the corridors on floors three, six and nine, plus those portions of the shaded apartments through which the section is cut. On floor plans 6 and 7 all interior public circulation spaces—corridors, lobbies, stair wells, and elevators—are shaded, illustrating how exceptionally small an area in the scheme these spaces occupy. Besides community ground-floor facilities, large community studio spaces are interspersed throughout the complex, and there is an 800-seat theater on the 11th floor.

The site is a square block in the West Village, bounded by the West Side Highway, Bank, Bethune and Washington Streets. The main buildings on the site were erected between 1898 and 1920, and were originally designed to house laboratory facilities for Bell Telephone Company; all have high-ceiling rooms, large factory-type windows, thick masonry walls, poured concrete floors, and fireproof construction throughout.

Meier's toughest problem was the transformation of this rather chaotic block of buildings into some sort of identifiable whole. The strongest existing feature in the complex was the central air court of the laboratory facilities, roofed over and used as a truck loading area by Bell. Meier made this relatively narrow shaft the unifying spatial feature, connecting it at the ground with three of the peripheral streets and to the small on-site park facing Bank Street. The design of this little park, the cleaning and painting of the existing exteriors, and the reglazing of some existing windows is the only new work on most of the exterior of the project. The new balconies which project from each apartment into the central court shaft fulfill city building regulations, providing two means of egress from apartments.

Inside, Meier's manipulation of space has ingeniously increased the amount of apartment area available by reducing circulation areas. In the ten-floor center portion of the complex, the usual baleful interior corridors have been eliminated on all but three floors—circulation to apartments in this section of the building facing the court well occurs on floors 3, 6 and 9 only. Apartments here are two-level units; the first or entry level on the corridor floor is relatively small, with a stair leading either up or down (depending on the apartment) to the main level, which runs clear through what used to be the old corridors, from window wall to window wall, some 50 feet—compare floor plan six with floor plan seven.

WESTBETH ARTISTS HOUSING, New York City. Architect: *Richard Meier—Gerald Gurland and Carl Meinhardt*, associates; *Murray Emslie*, project architect; *John Chimera*, field representative; Engineers: *Felcher-Atlas Associates* (structural); *Wald & Zigas* (mechanical). Contractor: *Graphic-Starrett Company*.

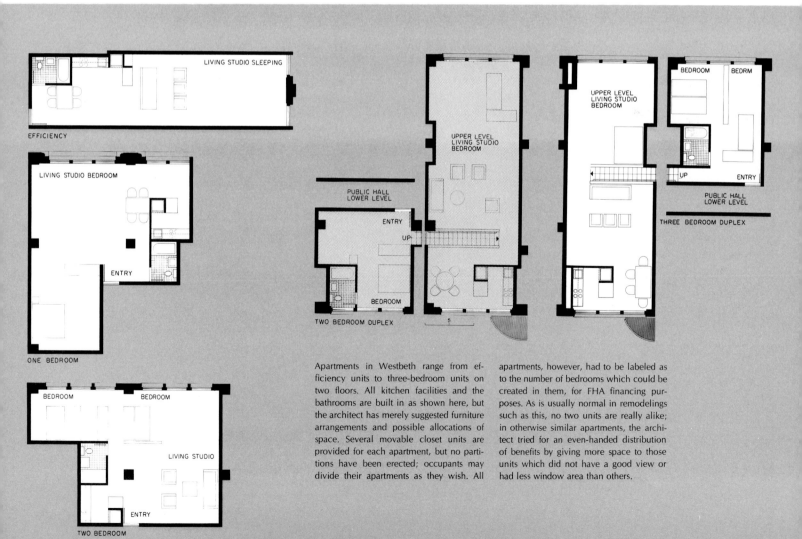

Apartments in Westbeth range from efficiency units to three-bedroom units on two floors. All kitchen facilities and the bathrooms are built in as shown here, but the architect has merely suggested furniture arrangements and possible allocations of space. Several movable closet units are provided for each apartment, but no partitions have been erected; occupants may divide their apartments as they wish. All apartments, however, had to be labeled as to the number of bedrooms which could be created in them, for FHA financing purposes. As is usually normal in remodelings such as this, no two units are really alike; in otherwise similar apartments, the architect tried for an even-handed distribution of benefits by giving more space to those units which did not have a good view or had less window area than others.

Large Scale Developments

Large scale residential developments have an affinity for the big city location: after all, it is there that the ready market exists for what the development has to offer. But the big city location has its problems. Land is expensive, which means that it must be used intensively in order to bring in the return sought by the investors, and this in turn means that, generally, such developments consist of high-rise buildings. Increasingly, however, high-rise buildings have become accent points among lower buildings or even townhouse clusters, thus giving both a new dimension to the development and a visual variation that helps to mitigate the hyper-scale of tall buildings.

In some cities the policy of "infill" housing has demonstrated how to get away from the bulldozed site by inserting new buildings among the old, preserving the character and existing scale of the neighborhood. Several such projects, all in New York City, where the New York State Urban Development Corporation and the New York City Housing Authority have both undertaken projects, are included in this section.

Open space is an ingredient of first importance in the design of these large scale living places—large enough, in some cases, to be small cities—whether they are within the city or, as in the location of Village Greens on Staten Island, within the city limits but in a suburban section. Equally significant, and of prime importance in how the project is accepted by earlier inhabitants of the neighborhood, is the relationship of the new buildings to existing buildings and to circulation in the area. In some instances, circulation is designed as a means of linking new and old by inviting the use of pedestrian ways as a direct path from point to point. In others, new street patterns, made possible because of the new construction, actually improve on existing footpaths and streets.

Architecture is an exercise in social organization. Size is not the major problem in a large scale development; rather the problem is to plan and design to human scale so that the size, density and quality of the project serve rather than overwhelm the people who live in it.

The very pleasant environment created for Nuns' Island is achieved not only by good design and planning, but by a varied and interesting "mix" of housing types and sizes, and by a park-like setting aimed at reducing traffic hazards and to encourage strolling. Architectural unity was given to the various types of buildings by similar materials (concrete, brick, glass), yet varied by having one material dominate for each type.

1 Even in its initial phase of 805 dwelling units, this town house and apartment development on Montreal's Nuns' Island is an effective and extremely well planned and designed "new town." This first phase, with Montreal architect Philip Bobrow as principal, includes a 12-story high-rise (with 204 studio, one- and two-bedroom units) for which Mies van der Rohe was architectural consultant, and a series of middle-rise buildings, 3-story garden apartments and townhouses done with Stanley Tigerman as architectural consultant. Metropolitan Structures, Ltd., the Chicago-based developers, with their team of architects and planners, have indeed created a handsomely housed "spacious way of life . . . amid woodlands and meadows by the St. Lawrence River." Plans call for five separate communities to be built over a 15-year period.

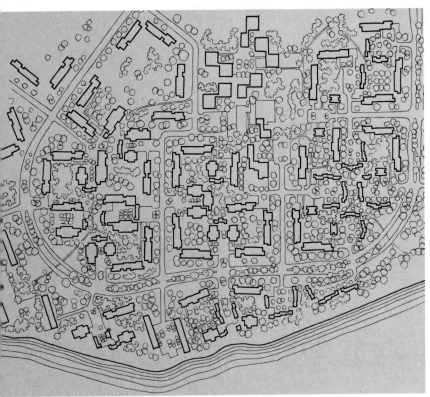

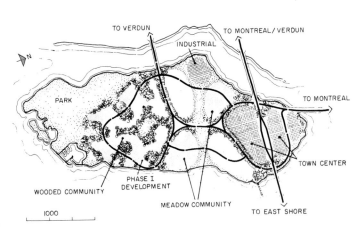

Zoning of the total island was planned from the outset; phase I, shown in plan and photos includes a community center, a shopping center, and a golf course. Phase II, with Edgar Tornay as architect and Donald Lee Sickler as consulting architect, includes a series of recreational lagoons.

NUN'S ISLAND, Montreal, Quebec, Canada. Owners: *Metropolitan Structures of Canada, Ltd.* Architects: *Philip David Bobrow;* consultant architects: *The Office of Mies van der Rohe,* high-rise; *Stanley Tigerman,* garden apartments, townhouses. Engineers: *Lalonde, Valois, Lamarre, Valois & Associates, M. H.,* high-rise; *Blauer Associates,* middle-rise (structural); *Mendel, Brasloff and Sidler, M.H.* (mechanical); *S.H. Lassman, M.H.* (electrical). Land planners: *Johnson, Johnson & Roy.* Landscape consultant: *Robert Meissner.* Contractors: *Cosec Construction Co., Ltd.,* high- and middle rise; *Metropolitan Structures, Inc.,* garden apartments, townhouses.

2 New York State's Urban Development Corporation has produced some notable buildings in a variety of fields. Among its achievements are the large low- and middle-income housing projects on a number of scattered sites in the East Tremont neighborhood of New York City's Bronx, credit for which it shares with the Urban Design Group of the New York City Planning Commission and the New York City Housing Authority. A different architectural firm was commissioned to design the buildings for each site, three of which are included here. The first, for which Giovanni Pasanella was the architect, consists of housing on two so-called "vest pocket" sites. His solution—high-rise, high-density buildings with split-level apartments—has been controversial but because of the ideas embodied in the planning of the buildings, has significance in any consideration of this kind of urban housing.

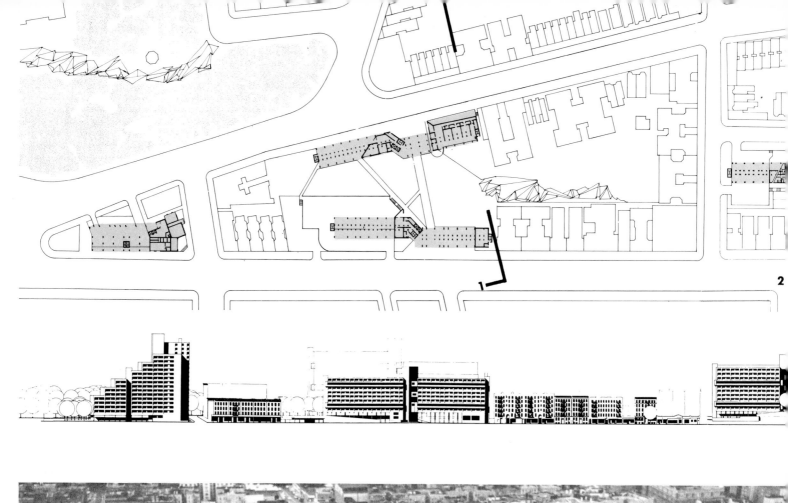

1

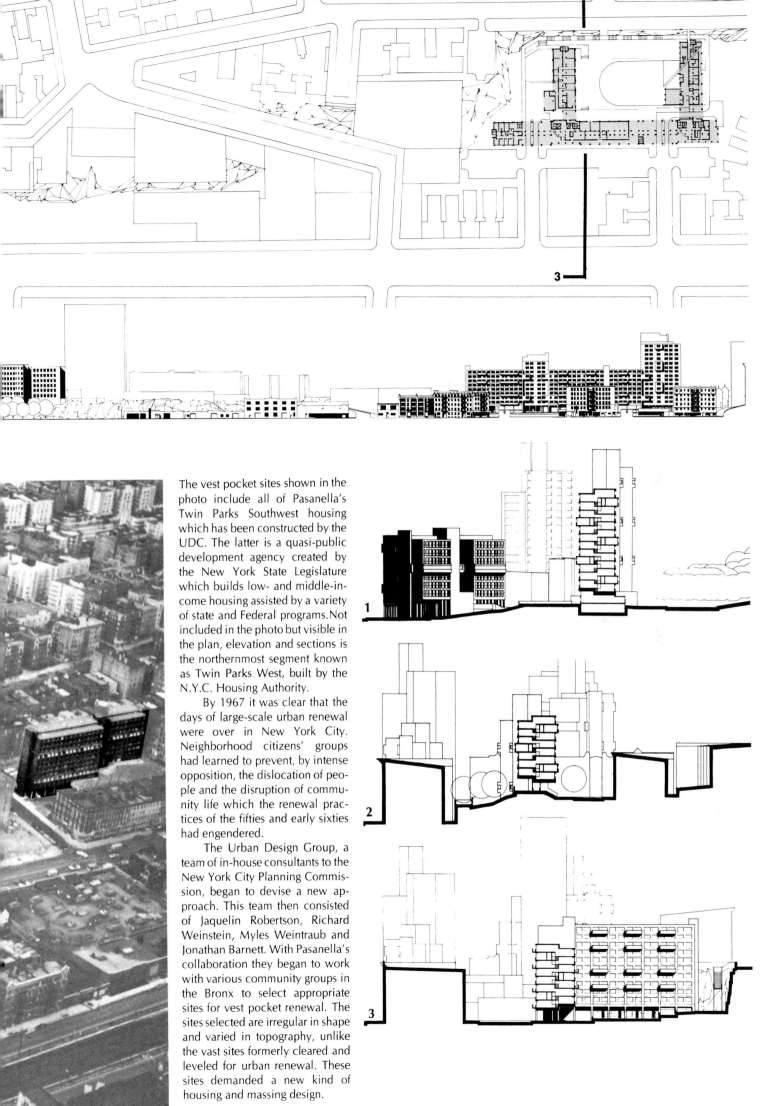

The vest pocket sites shown in the photo include all of Pasanella's Twin Parks Southwest housing which has been constructed by the UDC. The latter is a quasi-public development agency created by the New York State Legislature which builds low- and middle-income housing assisted by a variety of state and Federal programs. Not included in the photo but visible in the plan, elevation and sections is the northernmost segment known as Twin Parks West, built by the N.Y.C. Housing Authority.

By 1967 it was clear that the days of large-scale urban renewal were over in New York City. Neighborhood citizens' groups had learned to prevent, by intense opposition, the dislocation of people and the disruption of community life which the renewal practices of the fifties and early sixties had engendered.

The Urban Design Group, a team of in-house consultants to the New York City Planning Commission, began to devise a new approach. This team then consisted of Jaquelin Robertson, Richard Weinstein, Myles Weintraub and Jonathan Barnett. With Pasanella's collaboration they began to work with various community groups in the Bronx to select appropriate sites for vest pocket renewal. The sites selected are irregular in shape and varied in topography, unlike the vast sites formerly cleared and leveled for urban renewal. These sites demanded a new kind of housing and massing design.

Floor-through split-level apartments, in which living and sleeping areas are separated by a half-level change in elevation are a radical departure from conventional high-rise housing design. For what is believed to be the first time in any New York City high-rise structure, public corridors and elevator stops do not serve every building level. Rather, one corridor—and elevator stop—serves 2½ floors, saving 60 per cent of the public corridor space for redistribution into the apartments.

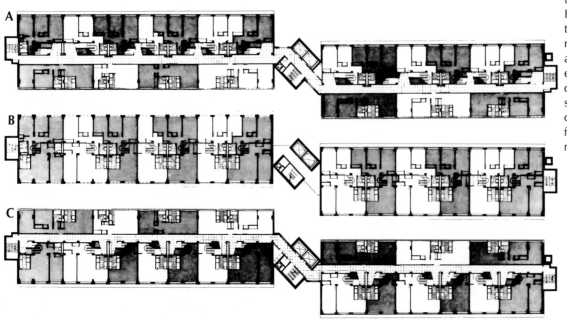

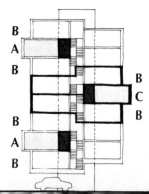

A large number of small apartments, mostly for the elderly, were programed for the southernmost part of the site because it is close to a major crosstown shopping street and bus stop and adjacent to a public park. To the north the next two sites adjoin with a park between, which replaces a former street. These UDC-built buildings including the apartment block on the fourth site have most of the larger apartments, and include community facilities.

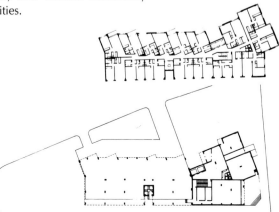

In defending the split-level dwelling unit type, architect Pasanella becomes eloquent: "Something better must be done for people than merely packaging them in an accommodation, stacking them up in units, stringing them out in modules. One's eyes haven't always seen, even trained architectural eyes, the wealth of evidence in New York for the existence of the 'counter-thematic' apartment type. The stereotypes of apartment/hive or apartment/filing cabinet are so powerful that we automatically withhold our interest, knowing ahead of time that it is bound to go unrewarded. But working out of an office in Carnegie Hall as I do, one cannot help seeing that many buildings in the neighborhood, always one of fashion and art, display façades which indicate apartments behind them of unusual sectional properties. A certain amount of serendipitous research has revealed other antecedents for our ideal housing type. These always embody characteristics which are displayed more in the cross section than the plan and typically are less the function of those details which produce the building's 'look,' than of certain efforts to achieve a proper ambience. These efforts cause some rooms to be 1½ times or even 2 times as high as others, or to relate to each other in partic-ular ways—apartments arranged on several levels as in our own split-level paradigm, or the more common duplex type. In such apartment buildings the capsule of space in which each family lives has taken precedence over the more technical aspects of the building process."

Apartments in conventional buildings usually have long internal hallways to bedrooms; kitchens and bathrooms buried deep within the building, and one exposure to sun and noise for the whole unit. The conventional building with its small number of apartments per corridor floor makes inefficient use of elevator stops, fire stair landings and other elements. For these reasons, Pasanella developed for Twin Parks Southwest and West his section element of five levels grouped around a corridor in split-level fashion. One advantage of this, as he sees it, is that the corridor is used more intensively, becoming safer as well as more conducive to social contact. Since the elevator stops occur only at every 2½ floors, vertical travel is faster for everyone. The floor-through two-level apartments have cross-ventilation and a change in elevation between the bedrooms and living areas as in the split-level house. The scheme accommodates one level units on the corridor floor.

Slightly different space standards called for by the N.Y.C. Housing Authority produced a less articulated section at the northernmost site. Fire balconies at the through apartments were added since the Housing Authority must comply with the N.Y.C. code, while the UDC does not. Both the UDC and the Housing Authority buildings are of conventional reinforced concrete flat-slab construction and are clad in oversize brick. Unlike the UDC buildings, the corridor floors of the Housing Authority apartments do not project.

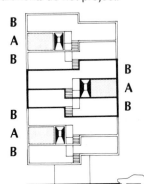

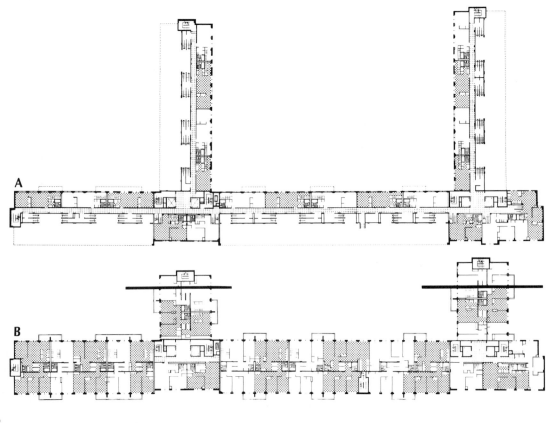

Gio tried to put Manhattan into the Bronx, says a UDC official who asserts furthermore that his agency will never build another split-level apartment building. Criticism of Twin Parks Southwest by the UDC revolves around two issues: the appropriateness of building high-rise, high-density buildings for families of low- to middle-income in urban areas where land values are not excessively high, and the practicability of the split-level dwelling unit in terms of the difficulties it gives contractors with no experience in this type of construction. Criticism number one is of particular interest since in addition to Twin Parks Southwest, the UDC is in the process of completing other high-rise, high-density housing projects in the Bronx and Coney Island. Because of this experience they are reversing themselves and now advocate low-rise, high-density for their future urban projects. In support of this change of policy, UDC officials stress that families should be housed near the ground to facilitate access to play areas, and to safeguard, by proximity, the community space. Ironically, the vest pocket housing projects originally proposed by the Urban Design Group for the Bronx were to be six-story semi-fireproof buildings. It was the UDC which insisted that economic criteria called for high-density, high-rise.

Criticism number two—the reluctance of contractors to build the unfamiliar—reflects a difficulty which innovative architects face. The UDC figures show that Pasanella's split levels were brought in at the same price per dwelling unit as the single level apartments in comparable UDC projects, which suggests that split-level dwelling units could and should become commonplace.

TWIN PARKS SOUTHWEST, Bronx, N.Y. Developing agency: *New York State Urban Development Corporation.* Owner: *Sovereign Realty Associates.* Architects: *Giovanni Pasanella assisted by Crane DeCamp, P. C. Wong.* Consultants: *Gleit-Olenek and Associates* (structural); *Dalton & Dunne* (mechanical/electrical); *Peter Rolland & Associates* (landscape); *Amis Construction and Consulting Services* (cost). General contractor: *Sovereign Construction Co., Ltd.*
TWIN PARKS WEST, Bronx, N.Y. Owner: *New York City Housing Authority.* Architects: *Giovanni Pasanella assisted by Crane DeCamp, Chris Wadsworth, John Robinson.* Consultants: *Gleit-Olenek & Associates* (structural); *Alfred Greenberg Associates* (mechanical/electrical); *Peter Rolland* (landscape). General contractor: *Carlin-Atlas Construction Co.*

Other split-level prototypes drawn to the same scale as Twin Parks Southwest and West: (1) Apartments for Unmarried People, Werkbund Exposition, Breslau (1929) by Hans Scharoun which was probably the first building to organize a split level about a corridor; (2) A Long Island split-level builder's house (1952; (3) Twin Parks Southwest for UDC; (4) Twin Parks West for N.Y.C. Housing Authority; (5) Early design for Twin Parks East by Pasanella (1970); (6) Dormitory project for SUNY College at Purchase by Pasanella (1970-1971); (7) Luxury Apartment Tower, New York by Pasanella (1972).

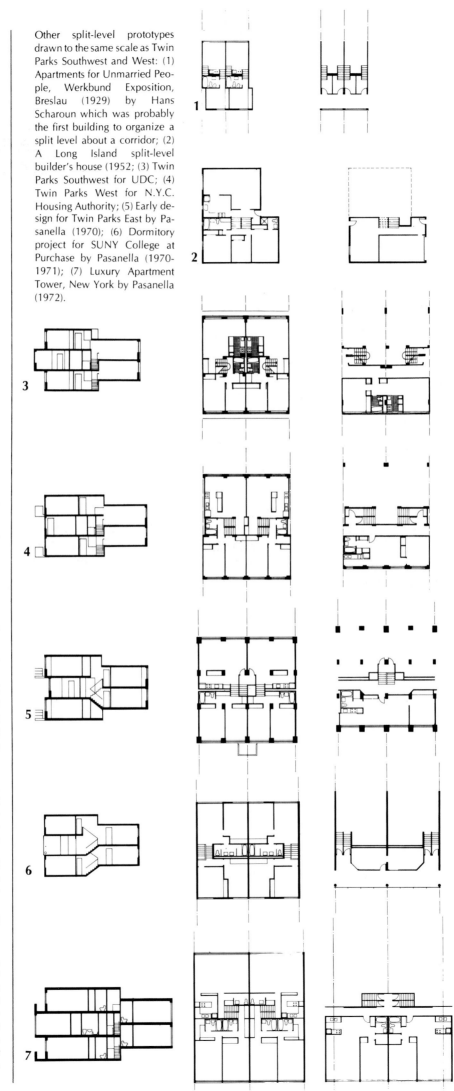

3

With this design scheme of hard edged volumes, containing small-scale private uses and defining large-scale public spaces, Richard Meier has resolved perhaps his most challenging design problem to date. Given parts of three adjacent blocks on an irregular site in the Twin Parks section of the Bronx, Meier's problem was to produce badly needed housing within a low budget, while reinforcing the existing neighborhood and at the same time creating an architecturally decisive entity.

The over-all massing, isometrically described on the opposite page, places the lower buildings so that they and the existing six-story

neighbors form public spaces of both intricacy and larger symbolic meaning. These spaces do not just serve for recreation and relaxation, but form a new nucleus for the entire neighborhood. Higher buildings face existing city parks outside the drawing's boundaries, and give a "sense of place" to the two major plazas, while carefully not blocking the sun, and producing an even greater density than required (523 versus 400 units). Approaching the isometric from center top (view at upper right, opposite page) a smaller scale common space has been ingeniously cut from one of the few rectangular block intersections by

the placement of the building. The lower leg of the southernmost building is straight ahead, and the large-scale plaza defined therein is about to be revealed. Entering and turning back to face the building opposite (view at upper left, opposite page), the full containment of this major public area, jumping a closed street and the basic block structure, is realized.

The other defined space at the right of the isometric is not so happy and is devoted to parking. Original parking requirements dictated entire open site coverage, but determined manipulation of grades produced a garage under the publicly usable portion of the

site. The relation of the southern-most street grade to the upper plaza and the lower garage is shown in the top photo overleaf. The architect was active in achieving a switch of an adjacent, "vest pocket" park designation to cover funds for development, but economies seriously cut over-all site improvement. The large-scale sculptured concrete benches remain as one of the few vestiges of a much more ambitious scheme, designed to lend a final air of humanity. The expanse of concrete, seen in the plaza below, is the roof of the parking garage and was originally to have been developed with planting.

Ezra Stoller © ESTO

This project was recently awarded a prestigious Bard Award for design excellence in public buildings by the City Club of New York.

Meier was commissioned by the New York State Urban Development Corporation soon after the concept of the Twin Parks projects, and was subject to some of the same growing pains as the client. While an attempt was made to establish standards and guidelines, some midstream changes occurred. One was a shift from boiler-fired to electric heating, which necessitated major ground level redesign. Realizing that an over-all, meaningful resolution was not going to be easily accomplished, the architect took initial steps toward problem simplification. Conventional poured concrete construction and traditional apartment layouts were an early decision.

This Twin Parks project was one of the first of many selected by developers choosing from those offered by the public client. It was chosen, said developer Fred De-Matteis, because of its straightforward building plans and the high percentage of repetitive, efficient simplex units (typical layouts are on the bottom of the opposite page). Single-loaded corridors, intended to light outdoor spaces and offer easy surveillance were partially eliminated for budget savings. The brick cladding was sensibly chosen in common with several other projects for UDC in Twin Parks, though this choice is far from the architect's previous inclination to ambiguous white surfaces.

In an effort to compensate for the clearly small, sometimes unworkable, programmed rooms (the client has since increased such standards), apartment windows are maximum in size, though this requires seemingly unreasonable partition contortions. Meier avoided a monotous cadence by grouping windows in large-scale blocks (as the above middle right photograph); and the glazing is pushed to the building face to minimize the detailing and emphasize the buildings as masses defining outdoor spaces.

To fulfill the UDC's role of bolstering and (hopefully) turning around slipping neighborhood situations, a tough site in a difficult neighborhood was chosen, and everyone involved knew it. The site sits on the borderline between two ethnic neighborhood groups. If any physical effort could turn down the burner, it had to be a major statement of confidence that these groups could live together.

Given the site limitations, this

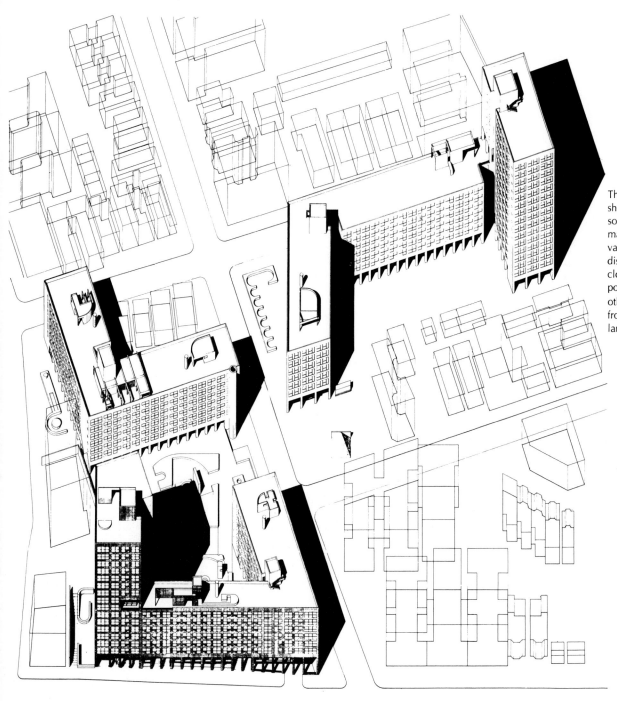

The over-all building massing, shown at the right, relates strong solid elements in a decisive manner and forms spaces of varied interest on an originally disjointed site. The more enclosed plaza is seen on the opposite page and above left. The other view is into that plaza from the smaller scaled triangular one, top of isometric.

housing might have taken the form of infill, but this would have neglected problems of social context and any natural assets. The architect knew that this stronger solution was required if any psychological dent was to be made.

While great effort has been made to relate to the existing buildings in scale, orientation, and roof lines—and selected street patterns have been maintained —as mentioned earlier, there is something new: a neighborhood nucleus. Perhaps the most controversial aspect of the design was the architect's intention that the exterior public spaces should be open to the neighborhood. In the large view, the architect has provided an open passage aspect as consistent with the public benefit. The general design success here might well be an example of how a building complex can become more of a success than any of its parts might indicate.

TWIN PARKS NORTHEAST. Architects: *Richard Meier—team: Murray Emslie, Donald Evans, Paul Jenkins, Douglas Kahn, Carl Meinhardt, Steven Potters and Henry Smith Miller.* Engineer: *Robert Rosenwasser (structural).* Landscape architect: *Joseph Gangeni.* General contractor: *Leon D. De Matteis and Sons Inc.* Owner: *The New York State Urban Development Corp.* and the *De Matteis Organization.*

Dorothy Alexander photos

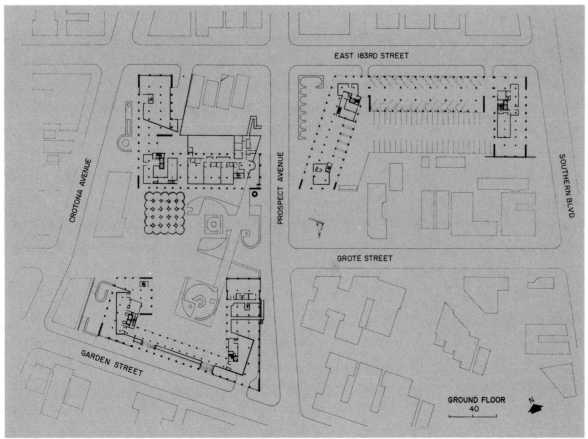

Ezra Stoller © ESTO

EAST 183RD STREET

CROTONA AVENUE

PROSPECT AVENUE

SOUTHERN BLVD

GROTE STREET

GARDEN STREET

GROUND FLOOR
40

N

Working with the most economical apartment layouts, conventional construction and repetitive window types, Richard Meier nonetheless made a strong statement at the larger scale into which the parts were assembled. Parking was partially accommodated on open ground floors (plan right) and in a garage under the plaza. The relation of Garden Street and the upper plaza can be seen above.

4 Twin Parks Northwest in the Bronx section of New York City is a project of New York State's Urban Development Corporation. Located on two of the 13 "vest-pocket" sites in this part of the city, these two projects are being developed as "infill housing"—new buildings fitted in between existing structures or placed on small vacant lots, to insert new housing in a neighborhood without large-scale clearance of the area.

The nineteen-story high rise unit fronts on Crane Square, and the location of Tiebout and Folin Streets was shifted slightly to enlarge this

The tower project of Prentice, Chan, Ohlhausen faces Folin Street and a small on-site park toward its main approach side. A steep escarpment runs all along Webster, and a part of the new work was devoted to building a new stairway up this slope, so pedestrians would have shorter cross-town routes. The plans and the section indicate the great complexity of the program for this tower, with zero- to five-bedroom apartments arranged as duplexes. One out of every three floors has no public corridor.

Joseph W. Molitor

CRANE SQ.

square in front. Both tower and medium-rise, central court project on neighboring Marion Avenue are modest buildings above their ground levels: no balconies, no undulating walls. Windows are small because glass gets broken quickly in this part of town. The designers intended these modest façades; they have placed their money on the site and exterior spaces, buying new trees, building protected grassy areas they hope will withstand hard use, and installing substantial street furniture in the form of benches and play sculpture. The Crane Square site has added a new path under the tower and down a steep escarpment to Webster Avenue much used by school children morning and afternoon. The tower provides units from zero to five bedrooms, and all the multi-bedroom units are on two floors, as the plans below indicate. This creates large inner-apartment circulation spaces.

These two buildings show the stages of development in a typical UDC project, and how the agency works with architects who, in the usual procedure, are hired for a particular project only after the UDC has investigated a project proposal for economic feasibility, community need for the project, and for its political and social impact. Clear resolution of these issues is never possible, of course: Community hostility to a project can arise at any stage, and cost estimates can get thrown out the window. For example, the Twin Parks Association (an organization of community forces) was the original sponsor of these two projects, but the financial structure had to be reorganized when the association could not raise the money necessary for investment at the beginning.

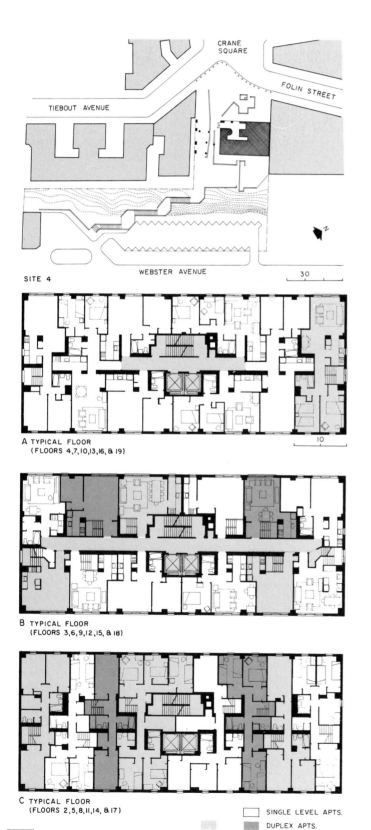

SITE 4

A TYPICAL FLOOR
(FLOORS 4,7,10,13,16, & 19)

B TYPICAL FLOOR
(FLOORS 3,6,9,12,15, & 18)

C TYPICAL FLOOR
(FLOORS 2,5,8,11,14, & 17)

☐ SINGLE LEVEL APTS.
▨ DUPLEX APTS.

Both projects have emphasized site planning, and this courtyard scheme is particularly successful. Landscape architect Raymond Schnadelbach has designed an intricate group of terraces and planting areas to meet the steeply sloping site, mixing concrete stepping stones, grass, and shrubbery with the masonry walls of the building itself. A large child care center occupies a corner of the building near Marion Avenue and there is a community room in the project; all of these apartments are on one floor. There are 334 dwelling units on both sides.

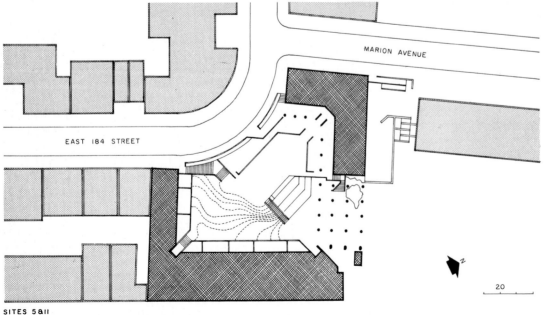

MARION AVENUE

EAST 184 STREET

SITES 5 & 11

WEBSTER AVENUE

20

After the architect who has been selected is given an orientation to the UDC, he is asked to evaluate the preliminary program that has come out of the preceding stage. Perhaps the program is altered, depending on the architect's opinions. In the case of these two Bronx infill housing sites, the architects began designs under the original program, and were well into it when the UDC and the developers decided to increase the number of floors in both buildings. The architects wanted the height of the courtyard building particu-

larly to remain low, and were required in the end to raise that building only one floor.

As the architect begins his schematic designs, a UDC liaison man with the title co-ordinating architect is assigned to the project. UDC coordinating architects are usually young people, with architectural degrees and licenses; and they are administrative trouble-shooters; they do no drawing, and do not tell the architect how to design.

At some point schematic designs are accepted by UDC, and final design/preliminary

working drawings can begin. These "vest-pocket" projects in the Bronx are the strongest attempt to date by the UDC to make a social impact on a major urban residential area.

TWIN PARKS NORTHWEST, Sites 4 and 5-11, The Bronx, New York City. Owners: *The Urban Development Corporation.* Architects: *Prentice & Chan, Ohlhausen*—project architect, *Francis C. Wickham.* Engineers: *Robert Rosenwasser* (structural); *Jack W. Barrett* (mechanical/electrical). Landscape architect: *Raymond T. Schnadelbach.* Developer: *D-U First Realty Co.* Contractor: *Kreisler, Borg, Florman.*

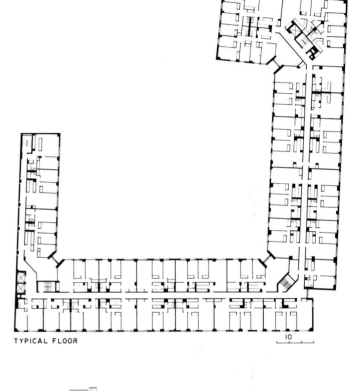

TYPICAL FLOOR

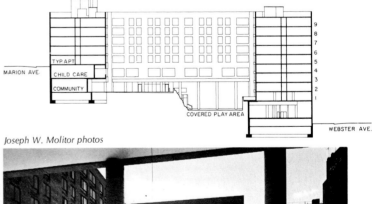

Joseph W. Molitor photos

161

5 Village Greens is a large-scale development on Staten Island, a part of New York City. Both developer and architect wanted to break the prevailing pattern of row-on-row single-family housing locally typical of such developments. They grouped the 2,025 units in nine clusters, maximized their individuality while retaining the economy of a simple, compact structure, and obtained a density on the 165-acre wooded site of 12 units per acre. Much of the site thus remained as woods for all residents to enjoy. In the model buildings such devices as projecting garages, decks, bays and articulated roof lines were used to break up the composition of the units. Subsequent units are somewhat less artful, but nevertheless achieve a refreshing variety.

VILLAGE GREENS, Staten Island, New York City, New York. Architect: *Norman Jaffe—Leonard Colchamiro*, associate. Structural engineer: *James Romeo*. Landscape architect: *Courtland Paul*. Developer and contractor: *Jerry H. Snyder*.

6

This project marks the entrance of Paul Rudolph into the aided-housing field in New York City, and the unique design reflects his usual fresh approach to architectural problems.

Given a site adjacent to and over the Jerome Subway Yards in the Bronx, the design includes one 40-story building, one 42-story building, and 36 townhouses. The plan is inherently economic, with the bulk of the units placed on solid ground, and an air-rights platform used for townhouses, parking, recreation, and open space.

The varied shape of the towers enlarges the vocabulary of housing in New York City, and is an innovative compromise to the circular tower the sponsor desired at first (Rudolph was opposed to pie-shaped rooms).

The townhouses vary in height from two to three stories, and are made up of mostly duplex apartments, each having its own enclosed court (see plan).

Parking will be on grade but covered by a trellis upon which vines will be planted to shield the autos from view.

Façades of all the buildings are of the split-faced concrete block Rudolph designed to achieve at modest cost the striated surface of his Arts and Architecture Building at Yale University.

The curvilinear quality of the total project was intended to reflect the street patterns of the area, which presently consists of educational, park, and reservoir facilities. Since the area remains so park-like, views from the partially enclosed terraces will be spectacular.

TRACEY TOWERS, New York City. Architect: *Jerald L. Karlan;* Design Architect: *Paul Rudolph.* Engineers: *Robert Rosenwasser (structural); Herbert Pomerantz & Associates (mechanical).* Sponsor: *De Matteis Development Corporation.* Contractor: *Leon D. Matteis & Sons, Inc.*

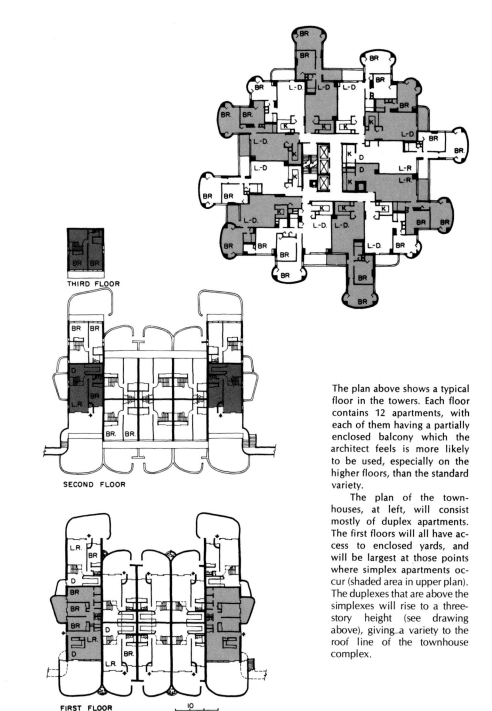

THIRD FLOOR

SECOND FLOOR

FIRST FLOOR

The plan above shows a typical floor in the towers. Each floor contains 12 apartments, with each of them having a partially enclosed balcony which the architect feels is more likely to be used, especially on the higher floors, than the standard variety.

The plan of the townhouses, at left, will consist mostly of duplex apartments. The first floors will all have access to enclosed yards, and will be largest at those points where simplex apartments occur (shaded area in upper plan). The duplexes that are above the simplexes will rise to a three-story height (see drawing above), giving a variety to the roof line of the townhouse complex.

7

Design complexity, previously something to shy away from in government-aided housing, was made possible here by the architect's innovative mind, as well as the revised fee structure.

The air-rights site over a train yard posed many problems, because some areas required more headroom than others. Frequent changes in site elevation resulted, which have been used advantageously to include an exciting set of alternatives in the circulation system, and a visually stimulating series of varying roof elevations. The intricate massing of the buildings is sensitive though, of course, it adds to construction costs. Savings from a unique wall system are expected to substantially offset the costs of air-rights structures, underground parking, and non-repetitive design.

Walls between spandrels are of hollow-core, eight-inch concrete block (3500-pound) constructed so that the cores form a vertical air shaft, open at the base, to allow water to weep. The interior will be waterproofed, and two-inch-thick sheets of expanded polystyrene attached by brackets. Wallboard will be laminated to the insulation. The whole process is expected to greatly reduce construction time.

HARBOR HOUSES, New York City. Architect: *George A. Diamond Associates;* consulting architect: *Herbert L. Mandel.* Engineers: *Goldreich, Page, and Thropp* (structural); *Arthur D. Benjamin* (electrical, mechanical). Landscape architect: *M. Paul Friedberg and Associates.* Sponsor: *Local 1814, International Longshoremen's Association.* Contractor: *Bonwit Building Corporation.*

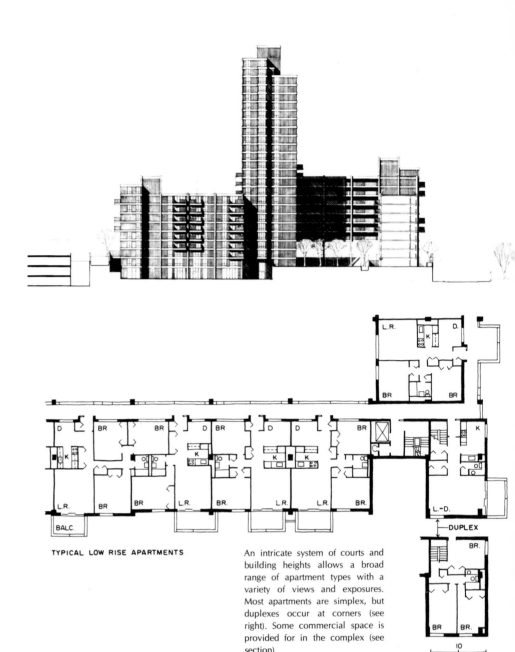

TYPICAL LOW RISE APARTMENTS

DUPLEX

An intricate system of courts and building heights allows a broad range of apartment types with a variety of views and exposures. Most apartments are simplex, but duplexes occur at corners (see right). Some commercial space is provided for in the complex (see section).

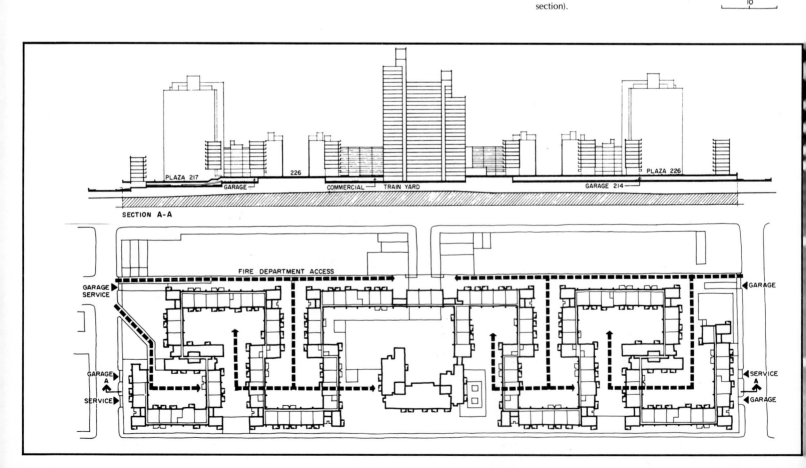

SECTION A-A

Sited on a gentle slope, many apartments have spectacular views of Upper New York Bay and Manhattan.

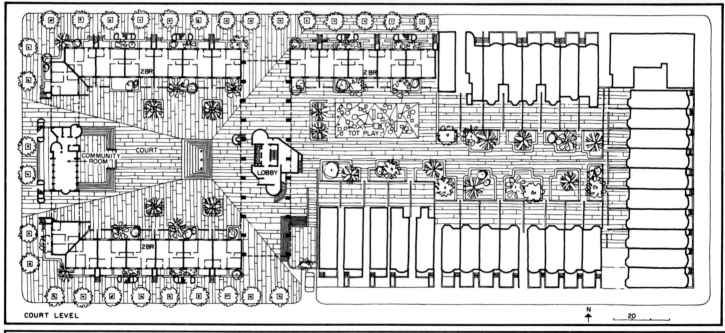

COURT LEVEL

N

20

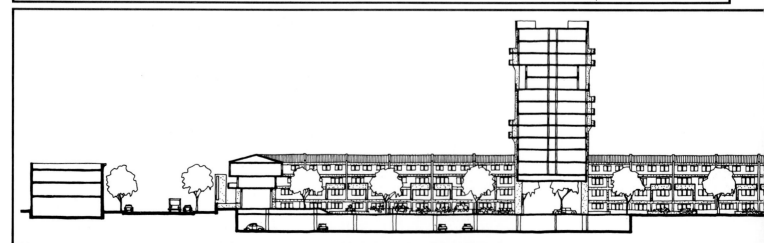

8

Typically, areas on the edges of slums tend to become the next slums, and in Crown Heights—which is adjacent to the hard-core slum area of Bedford Stuyvesant—the signs of this decay are already visible. The construction of Crown Gardens (cooperative housing requiring tenants to become financially committed to their neighborhood) was premised on sparking an internal and private redevelopment of the area.

The site is presently an unused, city-owned trolley-car barn, a blight to the neighborhood. A problem was to add to the housing supply in a way that would not make the existing housing obsolete. Within the remainder of the block, to the degree that the cooperation of owners can be secured, the plan is to integrate the rear yards of the existing dwellings into the over-all site.

The high-rise apartment building is located near the middle of the block, and raised 30 feet off the ground on a platform. Along the periphery of the site, four-story buildings will enclose a semi-public court and reinforce the street scale. All parking will be underground, below the court, freeing all open spaces to the pedestrian.

Access to the interior courtyard is through openings in the low buildings and under the platform of the high-rise. A community room located near the street, with terraces overlooking the street and the court, links the project and neighborhood.

The low-rise buildings have duplex units on the upper two floors, above two floors of simplex units. Because the lower floor is set four feet below grade, the maximum climb is one-and-a-half floors.

The high-rise has two non-typical floors of apartments for the elderly. These apartments have continuous balconies so that the older people can share this common facility if they wish.

CROWN GARDENS, New York City. Architect: *Richard D. Kaplan.* Engineers: *Robert Silman* (structural); *Peter Flack* (mechanical). Landscape architect: *M. Paul Friedberg & Associates.* Sponsor: *Crown Heights Neighborhood Conservation Corporation.* Developer: *Association for Middle Income Housing.*

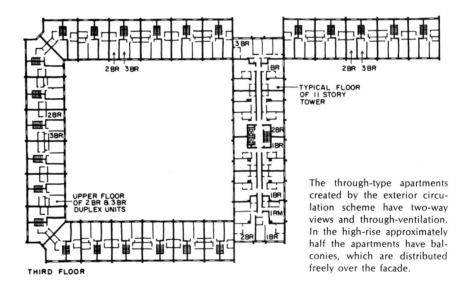

UPPER FLOOR OF 2 BR & 3 BR DUPLEX UNITS

TYPICAL FLOOR OF 11 STORY TOWER

THIRD FLOOR

The through-type apartments created by the exterior circulation scheme have two-way views and through-ventilation. In the high-rise approximately half the apartments have balconies, which are distributed freely over the facade.

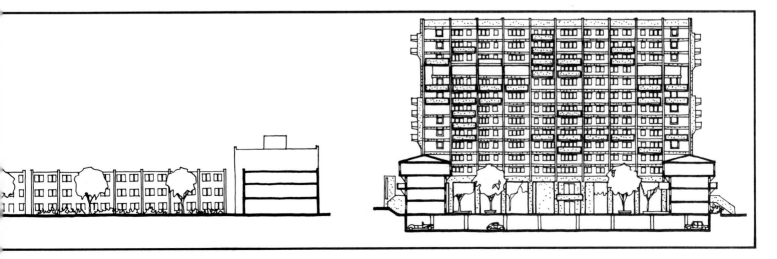

Shops along the street, above, and an outdoor cafe in the plaza, below, will generate community activity in the area.

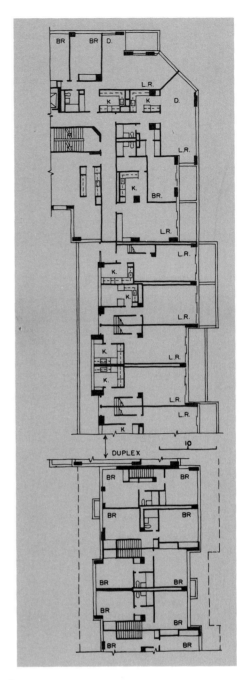

9

The east side of central Manhattan is becoming increasingly institutionalized with the rapid expansion of the many medical facilities located there. In order to bring people—a residential kind of vitality—back to the area, Davis, Brody & Associates have produced the kind of thoughtful design which hopefully will become typical in government-backed urban housing.

The site defines the southern end of an urban renewal area, faces onto a major crosstown street, and covers much of two square blocks. By convincing the city to close 24th Street (see plan, below), a through-block plaza was created, containing facilities for community participation. This space, along with the shops planned for the street side, will infuse the area with enough people to make it essentially self-policing and safe for the residents.

A series of ten-story buildings contains five layers of duplex apartments. Two high-rise buildings, of 22 and 27 stories, flank the low-rises and establish the city scale. These two buildings were designed with cut-off corners to soften their visual effect, and also to give better views of the surrounding city from the living rooms, which were placed at the corners. With this scheme, the architects have respected the city's grid system, but softened it somewhat.

EAST MIDTOWN PLAZA, New York City. Architects: *Davis, Brody & Associates.* Engineers: *Robert Rosenwasser* (structural); *Cosentini Associates* (mechanical). Landscape architect: *M. Paul Friedberg & Associates.* Sponsor: *East Midtown Community Housing Corporation.* Contractor: *Cauldwell-Wingate.* Lighting consultant: *David Mintz.*

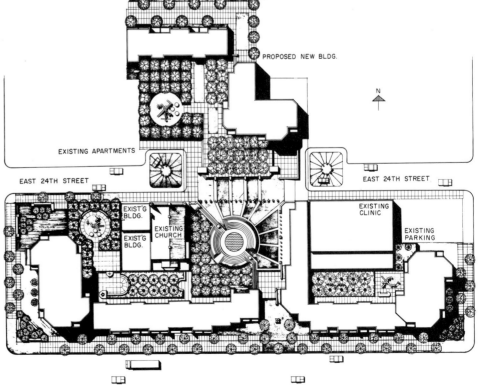

The richly expressed façade and carefully developed interior court create a pleasant space way from the street.

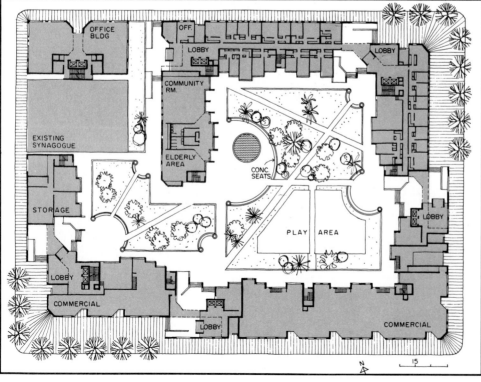

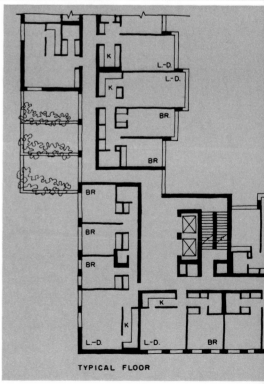

TYPICAL FLOOR

10

An older project many years in the making, Seward Park Extension has reflected in its design evolution a virtual revolution in design philosophy. Originally designed as a cookie-cutter type of structure (by another architect) repeated over the site in parallel, and, in its original form, disregarding existing neighborhood social and religious institutions (which, in the present site plan, survive), it became the first urban renewal project in New York City for which a "concept plan" was developed.

William Pedersen's fine design holds the lines of the streets and forms a serene enclave, away from urban inundations, surrounded by the project. Also within this fabric, an existing synagogue and a small office building have been included.

A carefully balanced mixture of townhouses and terraced high-rise buildings allows the complex to build slowly up to city scale. Terraces are developed as roof gardens, and, in effect, will retrieve the total land area for open space.

At maximum height the buildings are 22 stories high, with an average of 14 stories. Terraces occur approximately every two floors. Parking is handled in a garage adjacent to the site.

Constructed of reinforced concrete, the façades are of dark red brick, and faceted to allow each apartment maximum sunlight.

SEWARD PARK EXTENSION, New York City. Architects: *William F. Pedersen & Associates.* Engineers: *Hertzberg & Cantor (structural); Herman Scherr & Associates (mechanical, electrical).* Landscape architect: *James Fanning.* Sponsor: *Hegeman-Harris Co., Inc.* Contractor: *Hegeman-Harris Co.*

Many types of flats are included in the 560 units planned. The scheme is double-loaded corridors, with the maximum number of apartments oriented to receive sun, resulting in the interesting broken façade shown in the rendering above.

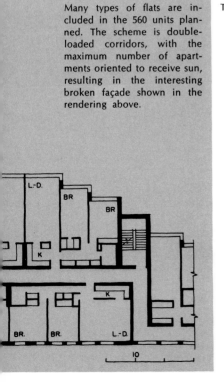

Terracing creates many levels of usable outdoor space.

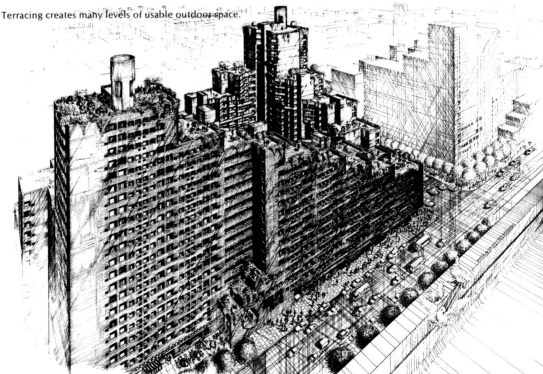

Condominiums and Apartments in Resort Areas

In resort areas it is essential that the demand on the land for development be reasonable, not excessive. Perhaps more than other kinds of places, the resort area needs protection if it is to continue as an attraction to people. Too many buildings sited with too little regard for the character and quality of the place are a modern counterpart to the old tale in which the goose that laid the golden eggs was killed for its contents: the return ceases when the source is overused.

If it seems paradoxical to have a summer apartment at the beach, where it has been tradition to have a summer cottage (though it may have been scarcely more than a cabin), or a summer row house beside a mountain lake instead of a whole chalet for a single family set among its own pine trees, today's fact is that for those who want the pleasures of a second home, the apartment or row house is the means of having them. But it is a fact with certain benefits: more people can enjoy the natural beauty and recreational facilities of such places without using a proportionately greater amount of land when there is multi-use of it; and the high cost of land can be spread, in effect, among many where it could be prohibitive among a few.

Whatever the form of ownership—many, perhaps the majority, of newly built resort area living units are condominiums—or by whatever means the second "home" is occupied, the occupants will find that multi-family living, even in a resort area, can be pleasant. The buildings can be attractive and unusual, and, in the most interesting solutions, each unit can appear to be an individual dwelling, with its own identity.

The apartments and condominiums shown here are in a variety of vacation places: at ski resorts, on ocean beaches and mountain lakeshores, and one on a sea island. Form is important in all the designs for these buildings, but recognition of the requirements of climate and terrain are even more influential in determining the design of—and of meeting the ultimate requirement for—a place in which, and from which, to enjoy the special qualities of a special place.

Joseph W. Molitor photos

1

The Palmetto Dunes Golf Villas, along with an adjacent clubhouse, are the initial buildings in a 2,000-acre resort development on Hilton Head Island off the South Carolina sea coast. In scale and materials they enter very agreeably into the lush landscape.

The architects, Copelin and Lee, have admirably provided the flexibility required by alternate ownership and rental plans. The villas were designed as individual units so they could be sold as condominiums. And their rooms are arranged so they may be rented singly, like motel rooms, or in suites of up to three bedrooms with or without a living-dining area (which may also be slept in) and kitchen.

There are three types of units (a fourth will be built later) which have good planning features in common. Each bedroom and living area has either a screened or open porch with a view over the lagoon or into a private courtyard. Each unit has a storage area which the owner may use in case of rental. And each entry is off a court so there is a pleasant progression from the large scale of the parking area to the intimacy of the houses.

The A units are sited along the lagoon in an irregular way that preserved as many oak and palmetto trees as possible and left spaces providing views for the two-story B units overlooking them (see site plan). The living areas of the B units are on the second floor to enhance their views. Because of the limited waterfront, the C units are in an inland cluster with views into private courts.

It is not only the small scale of these buildings but also the use of wood which helps them blend into nature. The vertical and diagonal siding and the trellises echo the strong shadows and pattern of the palmetto leaves.

PALMETTO DUNES, Hilton Head Island, South Carolina. Owner: *Palmetto Dunes Corporation.* Architects: *John K. Copelin* and *William M. S. Lee.* Engineers: *Dalton and Dalton* (mechanical). Contractor: *Graves Construction Company.*

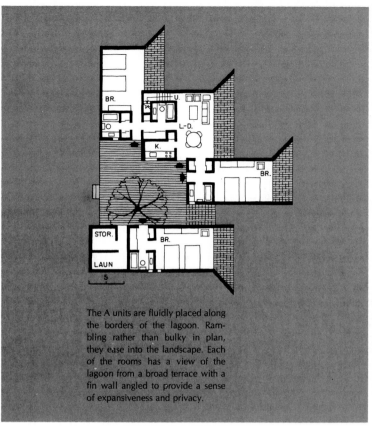

The A units are fluidly placed along the borders of the lagoon. Rambling rather than bulky in plan, they ease into the landscape. Each of the rooms has a view of the lagoon from a broad terrace with a fin wall angled to provide a sense of expansiveness and privacy.

Palmetto Dunes' B unit is entered through a small, enclosed and trellised court, or by way of an exterior stair. This stair enables the second story—with its sleeping balcony over the kitchen and the living-sleeping area—to be rented separately. The C units are reached by a trellised passageway and central court.

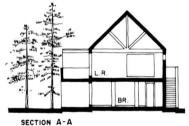

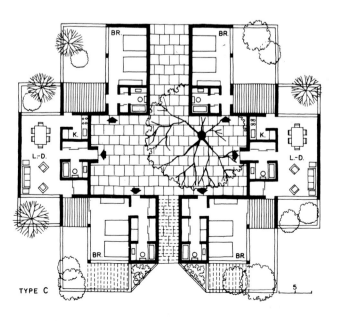

Thomas A. Abels photos

2 Architects Donald Sandy and James Babcock have gently placed Ocean House, with 84 apartments, on the sloping sand above the beach at Monterey, California, by using wood pole construction. Thus, the sand can shift and adjust itself naturally around and under the buildings over the years. Since one-third of the site, which Donald Phillips, the developer, owned, is public beach, the architects chose a solution which would make the complex seem as naturally and intimately integrated to the beach and the water as possible. The four buildings step horizontally and vertically in order to achieve maximum adaptation to the topography. They form a large "W" on the site, providing two spaces which open toward the beach and one enclosed space surrounding a pool. Every unit has a water view and direct access to the beach. Standard wood framing tied to the pole foundations allows the upper floor of each apartment to have a sloping ceiling with exposed beams and decking. The natural incense cedar, used for the exterior siding, will weather to a color sympathetic to the seascape and requiring very little maintenance. Black aluminum window frames complement the wood siding and trim and are themselves highly resistant to the effects of salt water spray. Black asphalt shingles are used to emphasize and define the stepped roof planes which slope toward the water. Covered parking is provided on the uphill side of the site, under the building itself and a group of simple sheds. Informal outdoor circulation links apartments to each other and to the beach.

OCEAN HOUSE, Del Monte Beach, Monterey, California. Owner and developer: *Donald Phillips* and *Ocean House* (a limited partnership). Architects: *Donald Sandy, Jr.* and *James A. Babcock.* Engineers: *Shapiro, Okino and Hom* (structural); *Reynolds Engineering* (foundation). Landscape architect: *Anthony M. Guzzardo and Associates.* Interior design: *Mary Elizabeth Phillips.* Contractor: *Barnhart Construction Company—Robert Chase,* project director.

GARAGE LEVEL

ONE BEDROOM-LOWER

ONE BEDROOM-LOWER

ONE BEDROOM-LOWER

STUDIO-UPPER

TWO BEDROOM - UPPER

ONE BEDROOM-UPPER

ONE BEDROOM - UPPER

DELUXE UNIT-UPPER

5

Seen from the southeast corner of the site which is also the highest one, Ocean House reveals little of the openness and rich scale of the side facing the water. Because the land slopes diagonally across the site and as the space facing the ocean narrows, units which are across from each other gain privacy since floor levels in each building are different. Units range in size from studios which have one exposure to the Bay, through one- and two-bedroom units with two views, to the deluxe units on the end facing the water. Those on the upper level have another bedroom over the living room.

Julius Shulman photos

3 Fifteen miles north of San Diego, on 70-foot high coastal cliffs overlooking the Pacific, architects Oxley/Landau/Partners have designed a dramatically sited condominium community of 51 single-family units. The residential density is approximately 17 units per acre which leaves a striking 74 per cent of the available land open—a desirable feature for residents in this particularly benign climate. The architects also created an underground parking structure that not only stores cars out of sight but raises the central portion of the site to provide overviews in every direction—especially toward the west and the ocean.

The apartments are upper and lower flats as well as duplexes and most have front and back patios on grade or terraces above. The massing of the units and their color and texture are the result of a thoughtful effort to complement the cliff edge site. All the buildings are clad with restraint in natural cedar shingles which give the entire project a welcome homogeneity and keep its highly sculptural character from becoming altogether too much of a good thing.

The interiors are thoughtfully planned and generously proportioned. The flats are over 1,400 square feet; the duplex apartments are more than 1,600. Ceiling height in many living rooms is 10 feet and double-height entry areas are skylighted. Upper-level spaces have sloped ceilings and exposed wood.

From beginning to end, the architects and owners have striven with considerable success to preserve the quality of the site and retain as much natural planting as possible. Where new plant materials have been added, the additions have been made with sensitivity and skill. The whole project has the pleasant flavor of care and concern.

SEASCAPE, Solana Beach, California. Developer and owner: *Westward Construction Corporation*. Architects: *Oxley/Landau/Partners*. Engineers: *Rick Engineering Company, Joseph Kinoshita & Associates* (consultants). Landscape architects: *Fong, Jung, Preston and Nakaba Associates*. Interior design: *Environs Unlimited*. Contractor: *Westward Construction Corporation*.

The meandering shapes of the buildings and their careful juxtaposition result in a variety of large and small courts. Every unit has at least 260 square feet of private outdoor living space.

BR.

BAL.

BR.

SECOND FLOOR

L.R.

U

D.R.

K

L.R.

BR.

BAL.

U

K

D.R.

BR.

FIRST FLOOR

5

Cedar shingles are carried inside to form a major interior finish material. Many living rooms, overlooking the ocean, have exceptional 10-foot-high ceilings and most are additionally fitted with private balconies.

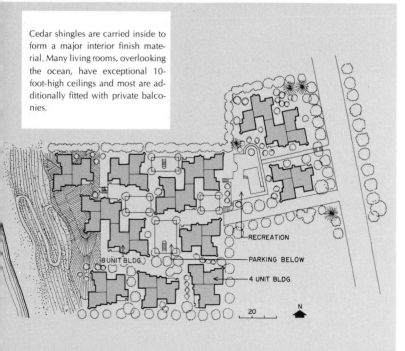

RECREATION

PARKING BELOW

8 UNIT BLDG.

4 UNIT BLDG.

20

N

All the apartment units in this handsome grouping are sited on flat meadowland and open toward views of nearby Sisters' Peaks. The rather jagged shed roof vocabulary, with its visual discontinuities, seems an especially appropriate response to the meadowland site and its mountainous surroundings.

Morley Baer photos

4 The Country House Condominiums form a small recreational second-home community at the foot of the Cascades in central Oregon. The buildings are situated on a meadow and grouped around a tall stand of Ponderosa pine that has been used by architect Donald Goodhue as a unifying design device. "The important thing we were trying to do here," says Goodhue, "was to give expression to the 'colony' idea—a group sharing a special place together, forming one discrete entity rather than simply a row of condominiums lined up against the spec-

tacular view through the trees."

The site plan gives special attention to pedestrian linkages between individual units and common spaces. The boardwalks are a means of controlling pedestrian circulation while protecting the privacy of the near units. They serve a social function as well by providing a setting for random and unplanned daily encounters between members of the community—a function that would be lost if circulation were more diffuse. Parking is contained within enclosed spaces, and automobiles therefore provide a minimum dan-

ger or distraction to pedestrians.

Individual apartment units are conventional wood frame with pine exterior and interior finishes. Their careful grouping takes advantage of the view while it provides a number of small-scale, private outdoor spaces that double as suntraps and windbreaks. Each unit is designed with a projecting bay window enclosed by a small-pane steel sash—a design gesture in sympathy with local building traditions. The interiors are planned as flexible spaces adaptable to a variety of preferences in the matter of furnishings and func-

tions. Almost all make generous allocations of space for summer recreation and especially for youthful activities.

COUNTRY HOUSE CONDOMINIUMS, Black Butte, Oregon. Owners: *Brooks Resources Corporation*. Architects: *Donald Goodhue of Hall and Goodhue—Bud Evenson*, project designer. Engineers: *Howard Carter* (structural); *Richard Lee* (mechanical/electrical). Space planner: *George Schwartz*. Interior design: *Tom Dearborn*. Contractor: *Keeton-King*.

SITTING

KIT.

DINING

D

U

D

L.R.

DECK

BR

185

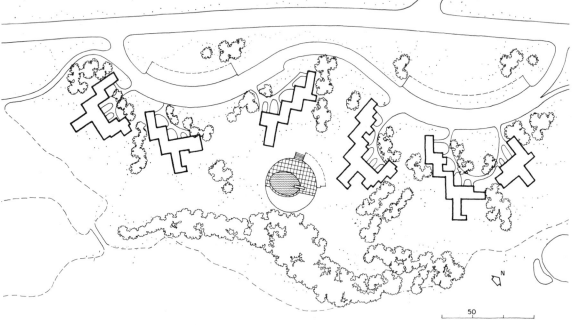

In scale and form and choice of materials, the 28 units of this condominium project look as though they belong to the meadow site. Construction is straightforward: conventional wood stud walls covered with rough-split shakes. The roofs are blue aluminum shingles over wood decking and exposed beams. Inside, the walls are brightly painted drywall with heavy, rough wood trim.

5 Snowmass at Aspen is a place for fun—some of the best skiing in the U.S. and a beautiful summertime, high in the mountains. But good design for such an area is carefully detailed work—for much can be gained by architecture that goes beyond the "Bavarian village" fakery to the real spirit of such a resort area. This cluster of 28 condominiums has, of course, its imagery—its forms are clearly reminiscent of the "mine-shaft" design that is as warmly familiar to this area as the shingles and great chimneys are to Cape Cod. But beyond imagery is function. For example, the broad planes of the blue roofs, while pleasantly random at first glance, are in fact carefully opposed to permit the heavy snows to slide completely off without build-up at valleys or chimneys and to avoid the problems of snow creep, dripping roofs, and overload. All roofs of the

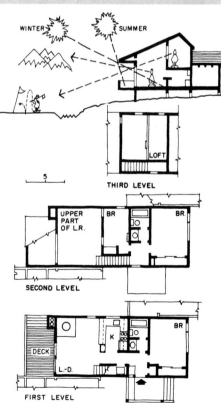

THIRD LEVEL

SECOND LEVEL

FIRST LEVEL

Robert G. Hadden photos

same slope are either warm or cold, to prevent ice dams. This opposing roof system also protects both entrances and decks—and the decks are open to the winter sun, shaded from the summer sun. Further, the roof plan creates, inside the units, a great variety of contrasting, bold and

small-scale, spaces. And this device, with the careful placement and juxtaposition of the individual units, eliminates any vestige of repetition.

The units are grouped so that the entrances open off court-like spaces to establish a sense of community—while the decks on the southern,

downhill side are arranged for maximum privacy.

On the downhill side are the heated swimming pool and cabana, and, just beyond, the fairways of a golf course. On the northern, uphill, side the buildings are shielded from the road by parking areas let into the hill.

SNOWMASS VILLAS, Snowmass at Aspen, Colorado. Architects: *Ian MacKinlay* and *Henrik Bull*. Engineers: *Don Simpson & Associates*. Interior design: *Erickson Associates*. Contractor: *Snowmass at Aspen*.

Robert Lautman photos

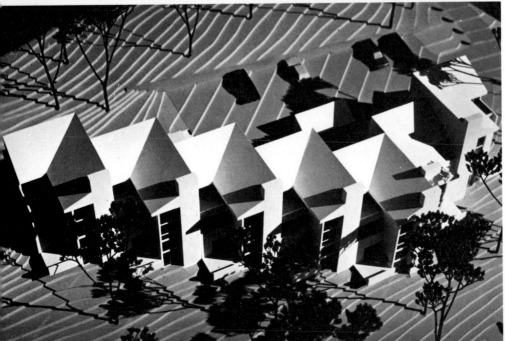

6

Beech Mountain, in Western North Carolina, is the highest (elevation 5,600 feet) ski area east of the Rocky Mountains. In addition, the area offers facilities for golf, tennis, swimming and horseback riding—a combination designed to make Beech Mountain an attractive year-round vacation retreat. In this resort setting, on a softly sloping, one-acre site, architect Frank Schlesinger has designed the 14-apartment condominium community shown here and on the pages following.

The apartments, equally distributed between two- and three-bedroom units, are grouped in seven pairs—each containing two apartments in a three-story arrangement. This pattern took advantage of the sloping site and minimized the maintenance problems and disputes so often encountered in projects with more extensive common corridors. It also provided identity for individual apartments by giving the project a legible, appealing scale.

The seven units are staggered in plan to conform to grade and setback lines. From the entry, the two-bedroom unit is down half a flight. This level contains bedrooms, kitchen, dining and deck. The living room, down another half level, extends upward a flight and a half. Stacked above is a three-bedroom duplex arranged to produce an upper level living room that overlooks a tall dining space. The plan shape allows the decks to be tucked away in the "L" for privacy. Each two- and three-bedroom apartment shares a covered porch equipped with lockers for ski storage.

Construction materials include stucco-covered concrete block for foundations and retaining walls, wood framing covered with cedar shingles for walls and roof. Major interior finish materials are gypsum board and redwood clapboarding for walls and ceilings, sheet vinyl on floors.

CHRISTIE VILLAGE CONDOMINIUMS, Beech Mountain, Banner Elk, North Carolina. Owner: *O'Keefe Corporation.* Architect: *Frank Schlesinger.* Interior design consultant: *Draga Schlesinger.* Contractor: *William B. Owen Construction Company.*

Lower plan shows two-bedroom apartment unit with depressed living room. Upper and middle plans show three-bedroom apartment, entered from split level stair. In this apartment, dining, kitchen and guest rooms occupy one level. Living room and master bedroom suite are located on gallery above to produce the tall spaces shown in these photos.

LOWER LEVEL   MAIN LEVEL |—5—| UPPER LEVEL

7 Orindawoods is a planned unit development which, when complete, will include 76 single-family lots, 80 garden apartments and 212 townhouses, plus a tennis club, swimming pool and small administrative building. These components share a steeply rolling site of about 185 acres in Orinda, California.

Market analysis suggested that the townhouses should be sold as condominiums and designed with the character and scale of private houses. Architects Mackinlay, Winnacker, McNeil therefore sized them at an average of 2,000 square feet per unit and designed them on two levels to conform to grade. The townhouses are grouped in clusters of four to keep them in scale with surrounding neighborhoods and are linked by a meandering pedestrian route that offers comfortable circulation.

The individual units are loosely strung out in plan and a central court takes a deep bite out of many, but adds a certain unexpected interest and planning potential. The court also provides an easy place to bend the plan where site conditions warrant.

Exterior walls and roofs are finished in Western cedar shingles selected for their weathering characteristics and their rough texture. Trellises are also in cedar. Windows have dark anodized frames.

The complexity of Orindawoods' massing grows out of the combination of flat and pitched roofs and the way in which attached and detached garages are played against the basic housing form. The over-all character of the project is unusually pleasant and the amenities it provides in terms of site and ancillary services are very welcome—coming as they do in a building type that so often in the past has not lived up to its expectations.

ORINDAWOODS APARTMENTS, Orinda, California. Owners: *Orindawoods Inc.* Architects: *Mackinlay, Winnacker, McNeil & Associates.* Engineers: *Shapiro, Okino & Hom* (structural); *Monteath & Krumholtz* (mechanical). Landscape architects: *Osborne & Stewart.* Contractor: *Williams & Burrows, Inc.*

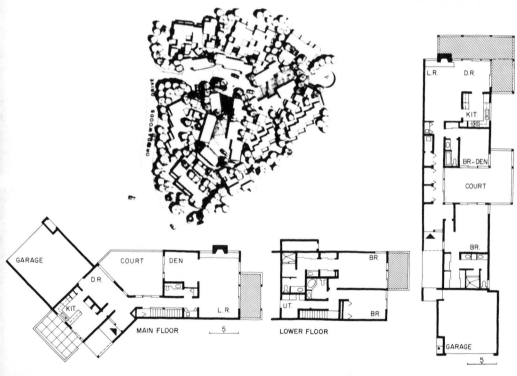

GARAGE   COURT   DEN
D.R.
K.IT.   L.R.
MAIN FLOOR   5

BR.
U.T.   BR.
LOWER FLOOR

L.R.   D.R.
KIT.
BR.-DEN
COURT
BR.
GARAGE   5

8

Originally built to demonstrate feasibility and desirability of construction on the sand dunes of the Oregon coast, this group of apartments has been so successful that six more units are now under construction and much of the adjacent area is being developed. The site is a narrow exposed sand spit north of the main residential section of Salishan, a developing community on a still lovely part of the central Oregon coast. The apartment buildings, closely clustered and connected by board walks, are designed in the vernacular of the beach: wood is used throughout—vertical cedar siding for the exterior, hemlock for interior walls and floors, cedar shingles for the roofs. The structure consists of pressure-treated fir posts, sunk in the sand and back-filled with concrete. The vernacular proved economical as well as appropriate to the beach site. Some units face the ocean with large windows, some with small, so that all have views of the magnificent winter storms of that part of the coast but at the same time convey a sense of protection and shelter—two major program requirements. The narrow, intimate spaces between buildings enhance this solution.

DUNEHOUSE, Salishan, Gleneden Beach, Oregon. Owner: *Salishan Properties, Inc.* Architects: *Church & Shiels.* Engineers: *Dean Athay & Associates* (electrical); *Edward Long & Associates* (mechanical); General Contractor: *Ralph A. Neubert.*

194

SITE PLAN

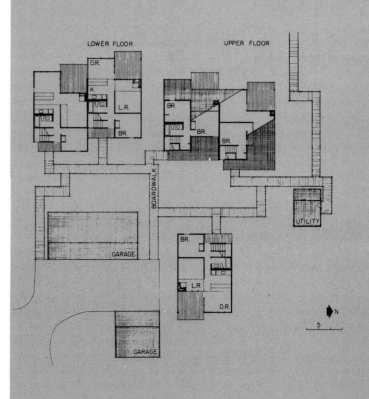

LOWER FLOOR   UPPER FLOOR

D.R.

K.

L.R.

BR.

BR.

BR.

BR.

BOARDWALK

GARAGE

UTILITY

BR.

L.R.

D.R.

GARAGE

N

5

Edmund Y. Lee photos

9 Constructed as part of the 600-acre Salishan development, this seven-unit wood-frame building offers three types of apartments, ranging from one to two bedrooms, with two to four interior levels and resultant varied roof heights, and offset façades. This consideration will become more important as other buildings are added to form the community.

An interesting piece of crisp detailing was created by backing the overhanging roof and façade shingles with painted trim. Partially enclosed decks insure privacy and add comfort to deck lounging by blocking strong ocean breezes. The shed-roof device works well in the interior space. Light, airy rooms reflect the expansive quality of a beach front.

SALISHAN LONGHOUSE, Gleneden, Oregon. Architect: *Zaik/Miller*. Landscape architect: *Barbara Fealy*. Consultants: *Mike Parker* (site); *George Schwartz* (interior design). Contractor: *Del Bennett*.

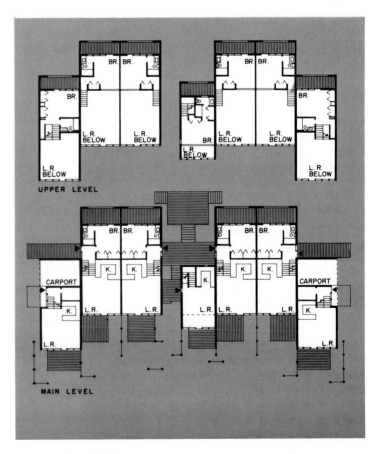

The informal cedar-shingle exterior helps to integrate the building with the rolling sand dunes and beach grass. The section shows the four levels of the two-bedroom apartment. Interior finish is gypsum board with some re-sawn hemlock paneling in living and bedroom areas. Ceiling beams were left exposed. Prefabricated fireplace units were used in each apartment.

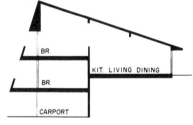

Apartment and Townhouse Interiors

It is a truism that there are no exteriors without interiors—and vice versa. It is not yet quite true, however, that all architectural offices have interior design departments, but more and more architects have added interior design capability to architecture in their offices. This kind of service becomes especially important in the redesign of existing buildings for new uses, but is equally important in remodelling for the same use. In this section on interiors are included examples of existing spaces designed for reuse: one is in a turn-of-the-century building, exceptional for the way in which the original character has been retained and yet modernized; another expands the actual space by creating a number of new floor levels; and yet another ignores outlook to create its own environment. Three townhouses are also included, two of which are brownstone buildings typical of many parts of New York City. In one of the latter, the interiors are based on a concept of plastic forms; the other opens up the interior to create a two-story volume of space, thus providing a view to Central Park for both living room and balcony bedroom. The third townhouse redisposes elements of the house to increase comfort, efficiency, and spatial character.

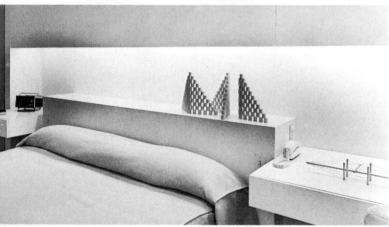

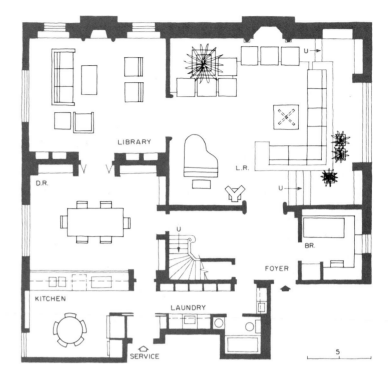

1

The renovation and updating of this apartment has resulted in one of the most unusual dwellings in Manhattan. Relative to most of today's standard apartments, this one is large, and is in a 1905 building designed by the late Charles Platt. In recognition of the architectural merit of the original plan and the handsome two-story living room, luxurious for New York even in 1905 (the building was designed as an artist's cooperative, where double height studios could be justified), both were left substantially unchanged. With due respect likewise to an old-fashioned curving staircase, the original lacy moldings, filigree window, balcony and ornamental eccentricities of the living room, changes were made rather to dramatize existing spaces, the apartment transformed with white paint, tile, acrylics and plastics, and rooms reclaimed from the dark, if lovely, Edwardian age and visually enlarged. A cool spacious shell of white walls (most apartments are painted every two or three years in Manhattan), white plush scatter rugs, clear acrylic tables and stainless steel for sparkle make a continuous backdrop for black-tie parties, flowers, books, art (the minimal sculpture is by C. Meadmore)—and children's toys. The apartment was designed to reflect a living style, and as a bright haven from the continual assault and battery of air pollution, noise and soot rampant in New York today. Plastics and synthetics throughout, with pyroceramic counters, vinyl cushions and tile floors, the elegant white-on-white spaces are childproof, stay in pristine condition and can practically be hosed down. Conventional Miesian furniture, formerly in the living room, was placed in the library and replaced by a wrap-around platform to provide uncluttered seating, focus and scale for the 20-foot-high room and to put to best advantage bookcases, and a major opening—fireplace, window or door—centered on each wall. David Beer, director of design for Welton Becket & Associates' New York office, was the architect. Contractor was Marshall Construction Co.

2

This Manhattan apartment by Egyptian-born architect Gamal El Zoghby is designed with such concern for living space and its sculptural manipulation that a host of drawings would be required to adequately illustrate its every complexity. Basically, it is half a floor of a New York brownstone with one exposure and party walls at each side. The interior design has been so intense that the original skeleton is barely visible and the environment that emerges is consistently abstract. The architect has introduced platforms to vary the floor levels, mirrors to expand the small space, and built-in furniture to give the design its sculptural esthetic. The owner uses the loft bed for sleeping, the paired beds below mostly for seating. A small kitchen, just off the entry, serves a built-in dining area behind the seating. The wall areas are mostly storage for books, hi-fi, clothes and personal belongings. Most surfaces are painted white but a powerful dose of color is injected into the design by blue carpeting on floor and platforms.

Invention and craftsmanship were required to assemble this extraordinary apartment. With the architect as contractor, and as carpenter, it got both.

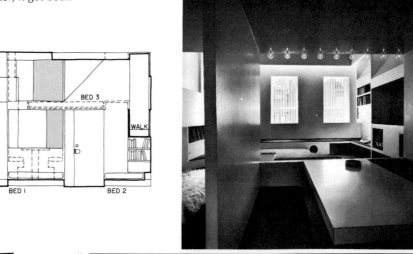

George Cserna photos

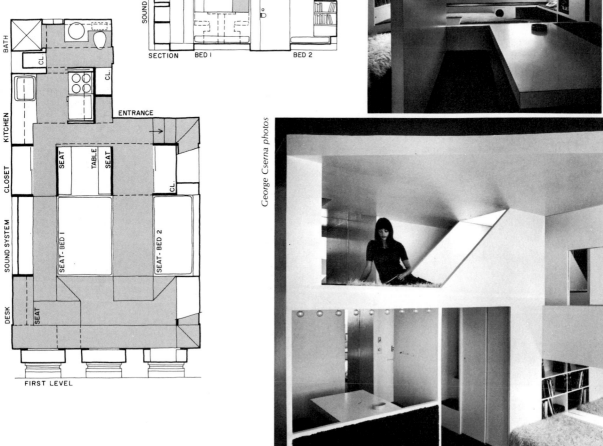

202

Nathaniel Lieberman/Todd Watts photos

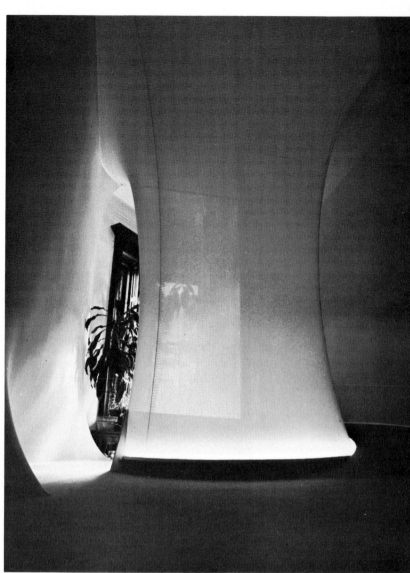

3

The parlor floor of the brownstone in which her sculptor husband, Vytautas, and she have worked for many years, seemed to Aleksandra Kasuba the perfect place for an experiment in sculpture for living. Two or three small-scale "environments" using stretched nylon fabric had convinced her of the potential visual delight of curved surfaces. But the execution of this project with eight separate areas (see plan) has exceeded even her expectations. Relying heavily on her husband for technical advice and criticism, Mrs. Kasuba has developed joints at floor and ceiling, as well as around openings, that effectively heighten the fabric's natural qualities rather than inhibit them. Lighting and light switches are so well integrated that one must know exactly where they are to find them. Beginning at the bay window filled with plants (left), spaces unfold both as distinct shelters and as intertwining elements. Thus the view (far left) from the entrance to the sensory (an "individual shelter") past the group shelter leads toward the eating area through a constantly changing tube of space. As one passes the group shelter (below), he can see through the opening (and through the fabric to some extent) the opulent three-dimensional rug (below left). Around behind the couch and movable tables is another surprise, the hemispherical sleeping bower of woven yak hair on bent acrylic support strips.

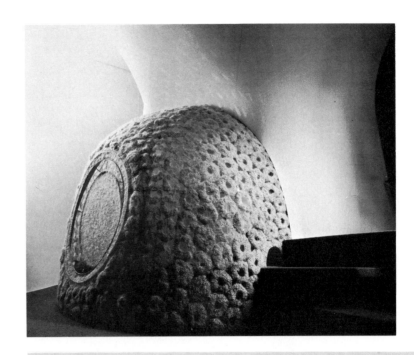

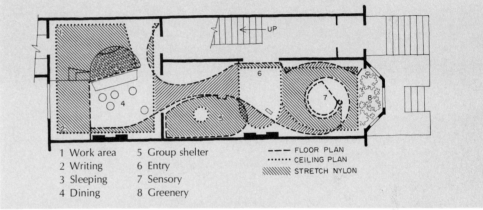

1 Work area 5 Group shelter
2 Writing   6 Entry
3 Sleeping   7 Sensory
4 Dining   8 Greenery

– – – FLOOR PLAN
· · · · · CEILING PLAN
⧹⧹⧹⧹⧹ STRETCH NYLON

4

Architects Robert Stern and John Hagmann have completely remodeled this duplex apartment on Manhattan's West Side. When they began, the apartment had a narrow, confined kitchen and no double-height space. The architects opened up the space vertically to provide a view to Central Park for both living room and bedroom balcony above. They also combined the existing kitchen and pantry to create a comfortable, eat-in kitchen.

"The use of curved walls," says Robert Stern, "derives from an orderly functional flow from the relocated entrance to living and dining spaces" and from a desire "to have the dramatic view unfold slowly to the visitor."

The owners are art collectors and asked the architects to provide suitable spaces for the display of various sized paintings and sculptures. The architects have done this, using cabinets and cases and recessed shelving with special skill to give the individual pieces sympathetic scale and background.

The apartment's spaces are orderly but flow into each other easily around curving wall planes. The high degree of detailing is consistent and intelligent throughout.

DUPLEX APARTMENT, New York City. Architects: *Robert A. M. Stern* and *John S. Hagmann*. Engineers: *Robert Silman* (structural); *George Langer* (mechanical). Contractor: *Garson-Bergman, Inc.*

Maris-Semel photos

Architects Stern and Hagmann retained the existing staircase but modified it by new construction to link the living room and master bedroom above. A bridge connects the bedroom balcony with a narrow terrace that overlooks the park. In the kitchen, the existing beam structure was left largely untouched.

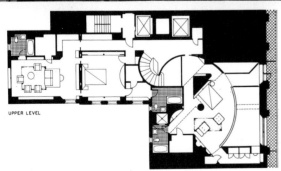

UPPER LEVEL

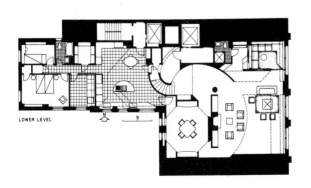

LOWER LEVEL

All photographs courtesy of *House Beautiful*. Copyright the Hearst Corporation, 1972.

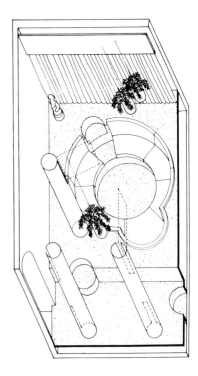

5

A typical Manhattan apartment posed some typically severe space problems for the owner and architect, Der Scutt, who, when not designing for himself, is a senior designer for Kahn & Jacobs/Hellmuth, Obata & Kassabaum, the prominent New York architectural firm. Spaces were boring and viewless windows offered no prospect of relief. Standard floor areas were thus turned into a totally interior environment and visually enlarged through purely architectural means, with visually expanded space for entry and standard 12-by-21-foot living room achieved using a consistent geometry and color scheme. Wall-to-wall carpeting and upholstery, related in texture and beige color, unify seating with walking levels, thus banishing standard furniture with its attendant clutter and standard scale. Tubes, enameled orange and yellow, were employed with similar ingenuity to heighten visually a low ceiling, placed to direct circulation from entry to living area and house stereo speakers and accent lights. Like built-in furnishings, the movable circular acrylic tables were designed by the architect. A small dining room, mostly white, similarly gained space through the elimination of clutter and use of light (reflected off white laminated plastic, acrylic, black vinyl and chrome) and was designed to provide museum-like conditions for a collection of artifacts displayed on fluorescent-lit acrylic plastic shelves, adding another important view to a windowless space.

The small library is blue-carpeted, with a built-in lime green couch, and is formed of squares, offering a cool contrast to the warm colors and cylindrical geometry characteristic of the living room. Lighting, for which the architect has received several awards, is inventively used to add character here as throughout.

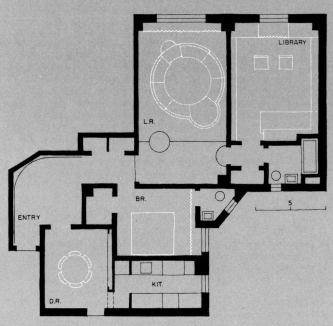

6

When their sons had grown and gone off to college, the August Heckschers decided the time had come to physically reorganize their townhouse on East 94th Street. With architects Joseph and Mary Merz, they decided to relocate the second-story living room to the first floor and convert the existing living room to a master bedroom. The third floor, previously bedrooms, was redivided to provide an intimate, informal living area (photo right) and a press shop for the owner, whose hobbies include fine printwork. The fourth-floor guest sleeping quarters were left almost untouched, but the winding stair, linking all the levels, was partially rebuilt.

A large built-in seating unit defines the formal living room, enhanced by its clear view through a glass wall into a landscaped garden. As the owners are art collectors, wall surfaces throughout the house have been designed to receive paintings and sculptures.

The final result is a series of living, working and sleeping spaces that are exceptionally comfortable and appealing because they have been well planned, well proportioned, and invested with more than the ordinary architectural concern.

HECKSCHER TOWNHOUSE, New York City. Architects: *Joseph and Mary Merz.* Mechanical engineers: *Dalton & Dunner.* Landscape architect: *A. E. Bye.* Contractors: *Gulli Construction.*

John T. Hill photos

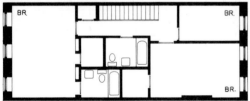

FOURTH FLOOR

THIRD FLOOR

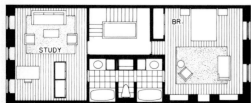

SECOND FLOOR

FIRST FLOOR

Combined living and dining space (photo above) is the ceremonial heart of the house. Built-in seating and cabinets are designed by the architects to complement the other furnishings, many of which are modern classics. Lighting is used with drama to highlight paintings.

7

The usual deficiencies of New York brownstones—narrow width and dark interiors—were present when owner-architect Peter Samton and his wife began renovating. They had a tight budget but wanted openness, daylight and as much flexibility in spatial and furniture arrangements as possible.

The width was fixed at 16 ft 2 in. by the enclosing party walls. The street elevation was established at the building line. But by demolishing a small existing extension of the building at the rear, and by substituting a generous window wall, natural light could reach deep into the waist of the building. Living spaces are therefore defined by furniture groupings rather than transverse walls.

Living room, kitchen, dining and work spaces occupy the parlor floor; sleeping quarters and playroom are below. A small, intimate court, at rear, extends the play space and furnishes a pleasant taste of outdoors. Completing this handsome renovation are two rental apartments above.

RENOVATED TOWNHOUSE, New York City. Architect: *Peter Samton* (partner, *Gruzen & Partners*). Mechanical engineer: *Robert Freudenberg*.

David Hirsch photos

In addition to flooding the main floor with light from the new greenhouse-like window wall, architect Peter Samton has added to the bright spaciousness of his renovated brownstone by a number of simple but effective devices: creating a completely open plan with different "room" areas defined by low cabinets; using the same flooring throughout; exposing the original brick walls; and selecting light, well-scaled furniture.

UPPER FLOOR   5   LOWER FLOOR

213

Index